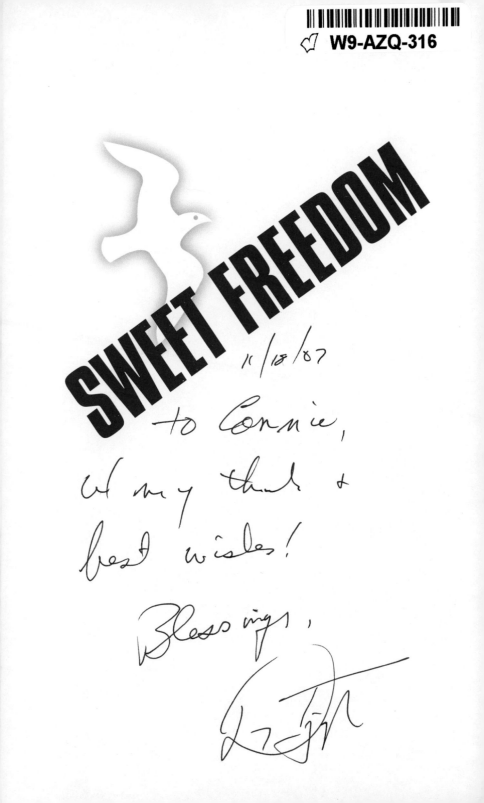

SWEET FREEDOM

11/18/07

to Connie,

wt my thank &
best wishes!

Blessings,

SWEET FREEDOM

BREAKING THE BONDAGE
OF MAURICE CARTER

BY DOUG TJAPKES

FaithWalk
PUBLISHING
Grand Haven, Michigan

©2006 Doug Tjapkes
Published by FaithWalk Publishing
Grand Haven, Michigan 49417

Printed in the United States of America
11 10 09 08 07 06   7 6 5 4 3 2 1

Library of Congress Cataloging-in-Publication Data

Tjapkes, Doug.
Sweet freedom : breaking the bondage of Maurice Carter / Doug Tjapkes.
p. cm.
ISBN-13: 978-1-932902-56-3 (pbk. : alk. paper)
ISBN-10: 1-932902-56-2
1. Church work with prisoners—United States. 2. Carter, Maurice, 1944-2004.
3. False imprisonment—United States. 4. Tjapkes, Doug. I. Title.
BV4465.T53 2006
365'.66—dc22
        2005030990

*This book is lovingly dedicated to the wrongly convicted whose
cases go unnoticed, unsupported, and unsolved.*

CONTENTS

Alex Kotlowitz is the author of *The Other Side of the River*, *Never a City So Real*, and *There Are No Children Here*, which the New York Public Library named as one of the most important books of the twentieth century. A former staff writer at *The Wall Street Journal*, his work has appeared in *The New York Times Magazine* and *The New Yorker*, as well as on *This American Life* and PBS. He is also the author (with Amy Dorn) of the play, *An Unobstructed View*. His honors include the George Foster Peabody Award, the Robert F. Kennedy Journalism Award and the George Polk Award. He is a writer-in-residence at Northwestern University and a visiting professor at the University of Notre Dame.

FOREWORD

Doug Tjapkes is my hero. Let me explain.

A number of years ago, I got a phone call from Doug. He knew of my familiarity with Benton Harbor and so wanted to talk to me about a man he'd befriended in prison who he believed had been wrongfully convicted. The thing about it was: Doug had absolutely no evidence. It was at the time all gut. He just believed in this inmate, Maurice Carter.

I was somewhat familiar with Maurice's story, especially the fact that he was tried by an all-white jury. The lone black juror, a woman, had mysteriously been let go. I'd also heard that Maurice maintained his innocence. But, to be perfectly frank, many of the prisoners I meet profess their innocence, often because it's tough for them to reconcile who they are with what they've done. Anyway, Doug kept on apologizing for taking up my time, but in his own quiet way wouldn't let me off the phone. He told me about Maurice, and then asked if we could get together. At this point, I usually beg off, mostly because, if I were to meet with every caller, I'd never get any writing done.

But there was something different about Doug. I think it was when he told me that he was a church organ salesman that I thought, *Okay, so this isn't someone with a political agenda.* We met for lunch and, by the end of that meal, Doug had me firmly convinced that the Berrien County authorities had convicted the wrong man. Doug also had me convinced of Maurice's upstanding character. I was on board.

This experience I suspect is not atypical. Doug, whose pastime is racing antique cars, is reserved and gentle in demeanor.

He apologizes for sending e-mails, fearing that they might be taking up someone's time. But don't underestimate this unassuming man. He has championed Maurice Carter in life and in death and won't let go until the rest of the world sees Maurice as he sees him.

But this is only half the story. In his quest for justice, Doug found a friend, someone with whom he could share his doubts and hopes, someone whom he could lean on (and who in turn could lean on Doug), someone whom Doug depended on and who depended on Doug. That was Maurice. It was a remarkable friendship. Two men from polar opposite backgrounds. Two men with no shared history. Two men who met simply by chance, and who had a visceral sense that each could trust the other. Shortly after Maurice got out of prison, I visited him and Doug. Maurice, who was ailing, leaned on Doug, both literally and figuratively. They chuckled at private jokes. Doug needled Maurice about taking care of himself, and Maurice needled Doug about taking care of his family. It is one of the most profound and heartfelt friendships I've ever encountered. I learned from it. I drew strength from its deep well of faith and loyalty. I was inspired by Doug's and Maurice's generosity of spirit.

This is the story of an accidental friendship and of one man's courageous, unwavering campaign to free his friend, to get the rest of us to see what he so clearly saw, to know what he so clearly knew: that Maurice Carter was innocent. This is a powerful, moving tale, one from which we can all learn, and one that should serve as a template for the rest of us. It is a story of crossing boundaries, of reaching out beyond the familiar, and of fighting for what is right and just. We all have much to learn from Doug Tjapkes ... and Maurice Carter.

Alex Kotlowitz

PREFACE

This book is not a novel, and yet some of the names in our story are fictitious.

It's a simple situation, really. Because we contend that Maurice Carter was innocent, it would logically follow that someone else committed the crime in 1973 that resulted in his arrest and imprisonment. The author, and several others who have worked on this case, believe they know the identity of the shooter. They also believe that many others in the inner city of Benton Harbor know and are concealing his identity.

This is an integral part of our story and must not be left out. However, based on the premise that all persons are innocent until proven guilty, we have chosen to use aliases for all persons remotely involved in that particular segment of our account. Any resemblance to names of real people is purely unintentional.

ACKNOWLEDGMENTS

In my first draft, I unwisely started ticking off the names of heroes as I thought of them. Sage editor and adviser Louann Werksma finally cried "halt," and suggested that the list be published separately. After two pages of names, I realized that I had hardly begun, and the task was impossible.

Ten years ago Maurice Carter could have easily prepared a simple, rather small list of heroes. By the time of his passing, the number would easily reach into the hundreds.

There are all the obvious heroes, such as leaders and participants of the Innocence Projects, the celebrities, the attorneys, family members of Maurice, his close friends, his supporters, and the members of the citizens committee.

But I also think of these unlikely categories: caregivers, children, and inmates. Especially inmates.

There was the nurse's aide from the Duane L. Waters Prison Hospital who secretly sent e-mail messages to me, asking what she could do to help, assuring me that she would watch out for this special patient. I know there were others in all of the medical centers where he was treated.

The head attorney for Maurice Carter is no more a hero than the youngest singer in Sherry Merz's Kids' Choir who faithfully prayed for his release every week.

Dr. Rubin "Hurricane" Carter is no more a hero than Maurice Carter's bunkie who most certainly saved a life by calling my wife Marcia when it became apparent that Maurice was too sick to be in the general population.

A Christian inmate had met Maurice Carter in earlier years, so when he was briefly returned to Coldwater to spend time in the medical unit, this kind man added the daily care of Maurice to his list of personal responsibilities.

I know of at least three inmate prayer groups in three widely scattered locations in Michigan that regularly asked God to bless Maurice, keep him in good health, and grant him his freedom.

And so I pay tribute to anyone, everyone, who supported the effort to free Maurice Carter, perhaps in some way that seemed trivial or meaningless. I assure you that nothing was small or insignificant in the eyes of God.

Acknowledgments should also include those who persuaded me to chronicle these events. Many people, especially family and close friends, suggested that I write a book, or a magazine series, or a movie script. But four people persisted until I did something about it, and I would be remiss if I did not give them credit.

Tom Beyer and I began our days together in the radio broadcasting business forty-five years ago. Our friendship has survived storms in both of our lives. He has always given more praise to my writing than it deserved, and he was relentless in pressuring for this book.

Evan Reinders was my brother-in-law for a few short years until a tragic accident claimed the life of my only sister. We still regard each other as brothers-in-law, and our friendship has deepened over the years. Sensing there was a powerful story here, Evan was the force behind the start of a daily chronicle of events in June, 2001, without which this book could not have been written.

Ron Frantz is the Prosecuting Attorney for Ottawa County, in the State of Michigan. He will be the first to admit that he had some misgivings about the Maurice Carter story when I began to share its details in our Saturday noon luncheon meeting for Studebaker drivers. Seeing it through the eyes of a prosecutor, in recent years he has been insistent that I write down the details of this saga.

Dirk Wierenga is my publisher, and this book was at the top of my procrastination list until Dirk read a newspaper account of the Carter-Tjapkes relationship. His immediate instincts told him this was book material, and he encouraged me to give it a try. I demurred, arguing that I was an old radio news writer, not a book author. I'm grateful now that he didn't give up. And that I didn't, either.

The book publishing business is a new world for me. This experience of book writing, my first, has shown me that there are two key people in the process. I believe that the book editor and the page layout professional who must decipher all of the edit notes, marks and scribbles, do as much or more than the author to reach the goal of a finished product. I am indebted to editor **Louann Werksma** and production manager **Ginny McFadden** at FaithWalk Publishing, not only for their premier workmanship but also their gracious spirits.

OCTOBER 2004

Maurice Carter was dead.

The man who had demanded almost every minute of every hour of every day of my life for the past three months was breathing no more. It wasn't even necessary to remove all of the pumps and tubes and paraphernalia that battled to keep him with us. God called him home at the appointed time.

I hardly listened to the pastor preaching the funeral sermon. The preacher was saying "Amen" too often. Amen. Amen? Amen. Even when it didn't fit in a sentence. Amen. Maurice Carter was dead. Amen. I tuned out the sermon.

I barely looked at the body in the casket which, after the artifice of some well intentioned embalmer, bore little resemblance to my brother Maurice.

I could shed no more tears.

So what's the deal, Lord? Is this your answer to our prayers? It's not exactly what we had in mind!

Maurice Carter and I shared a dream. He would get a new liver, and he and I would work side-by-side to provide hope for prisoners in the name of Christ.

For the past decade Maurice Carter had been on my mind, and very much a part of my life. For the past three months, since his release from prison, Maurice Carter and all the challenges related to his newfound freedom, and the problems related to his advanced liver disease, had dominated the lives of everyone in my family.

I first sensed that our just realized dream was turning into a nightmare when I paid a call to Maurices's nursing home on Thursday, October 21, 2004. I was never quite able to get used to his health setbacks. I could not suppress the feeling of alarm when Maurice barely responded. This was one of those days, and it was happening far too often. Was this due to medication problems again, was the hepatitis C running rampant, or was his relentless staphylococcus infection making its move? Or all of the above?

Placing my hand on his shoulder, I was able to rouse him enough to communicate the good news that a volunteer physician had completed the paperwork seeking an evaluation for a new liver. There was a slight grin, and he allowed that he was ready. He drifted off, and we could communicate no more. As I departed, I made certain that he heard our usual sign off: "I love you."

I leaned over to hear him whisper, "I love you."

That was his final message to me.

All the king's horses and all the king's men at Spectrum Health in Grand Rapids couldn't put Humpty Dumpty back together again.

Four days later I sat at the computer to give Maurice Carter supporters around the world another e-mail update, the saddest in the ten years that we were brothers.

Subject: Gone Home
Message: Maurice Henry Carter
             March 29, 1944—October 24, 2004

I later learned that he died after midnight. The death certificate reads October 25, 2004.

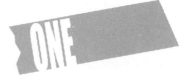

MARCH 2003

You're yanking my chain, Lord, right? This dude isn't going to run off with my car, is he? After you and I have come along this far? Give me a break!

I sat alone in a small home in the heart of Benton Harbor, Michigan. In case you're not aware of it, Benton Harbor is predominantly black. I'm white.

Aaron McFee, aka Dawg, had left me sitting in his mother's house on London Avenue while he borrowed my car to go in search of his "uncle," Deven Williams, aka Matty.

Dawg and Mattty had been having a vicious fight via telephone when I arrived. The language, while common on the streets of the inner city, was not what my ears were accustomed to hearing in the conservative, white, Dutch, Christian-Reformed-church-influenced community I hailed from.

My parents and their friends didn't use words like that in our simple upstairs apartment over a neighborhood grocery store in Muskegon, Michigan, where I grew up in the 1930s and 1940s. I don't think we were even aware that such words existed. As a young radio news reporter in the 1960s and 1970s, I quickly became exposed to another side of life where I did encounter that kind of language. But in my sunset years I've been selling church organs. Such vulgarity is nonexistent in quiet rectory offices or in darkened weekday church sanctuaries.

Back to the 'hood.

I had made the 80-mile drive because Dawg's Uncle Matty had assured Dawg that he would talk to me about the shooting of white off-duty police officer Tom Schadler in Benton Harbor back in December, 1973. I was not only intent on getting Maurice Carter out of prison: I wanted to clear his record.

I hated the drive and, feeling a bit of tension, found myself regularly checking the rearview mirror. Benton Harbor looked like a disaster area. Boarded-up buildings, restless people milling around houses that should have been condemned years ago, streets pocked with potholes, overgrown grass in front of shabby public schools, a smoky half-barrel along the street with a home-made sign offering "Bar-B-Q." If I were smart I'd buy some and take it home, undoubtedly to discover flavors unlike any I'd tasted before.

Finding Dawg at home was, at least, a small step forward. The last time I had made the drive based on a similar promise, neither Dawg nor Matty showed up. There were no apologies, either. I found myself in a strange new culture, a different community where my values, expectations, and traditions seemed out of place.

"He thinks you're a cop," Dawg informed me. He then returned to the telephone and unleashed a string of profanity on Matty that might have made the walls blush. He clicked off the wireless phone. "He refuses to let the two of us pick him up. I'm going to have to do it alone. Give me the keys to your car." I handed them over.

Keep in mind that I had just purchased this 2000 Toyota Avalon a few months before. It was a new car to me and it was a wonderful machine. I had only recently met Dawg and, while I believed he was a good guy, Maurice Carter told me from behind his prison bars that I was a sap, being sucked in by a con man.

Well, maybe I was this time. Maybe I would not see Dawg (who was unemployed and had several open warrants against him for unpaid child support) or my Avalon ever again.

Dawg assured me that the party store parking lot where Matty would be drinking was just a few blocks away. He would return in a few minutes. The time dragged as I paced through the tiny living room. I found myself rather secretly looking at all the family pictures on shelves and tabletops. I don't know why it surprised me that people who live in the ghetto have family and friends and fun times, too. A few minutes turned into thirty.

That's when the praying got pretty serious. What if the homeowner or her relatives came home and discovered this white man alone in the house? What if Dawg just took off? If I prematurely called the police and there was nothing amiss, the cops would certainly put him behind bars. And the tenuous relationship I had worked so hard to cultivate would dissipate in a millisecond. Should I bet on the outcome? Would Matty deliver the goods if he did show up?

My car appeared in the alley behind the little white house. *Thank you, Lord!*

Matty was a mess. He stumbled drunkenly out of the car, and it appeared that he had been drinking for so long that he was no longer able to control his faculties. His legs, arms, and face twitched. He had very few teeth. The combination of his lack of dentures, too much alcohol, and his inner-city forms of expression resulted in a string of lingo that I couldn't understand.

It was as if I were a newsman again, trying to interview someone from a foreign land. Dawg would serve as the interpreter. The conversation was painstakingly slow, but fruitful.

I had hit pay dirt.

TWO

JUNE 1997

"Collect call from Maurice Carter."

My wife Marcia was listening to the automated telephone message from the Michigan Department of Corrections Lakeland Facility in Coldwater. She could see by the look on my face that I wasn't excited about taking this call, or any other, from another inmate.

It was all my own doing. I had befriended a prisoner a couple of years before who staunchly proclaimed his innocence. I began donating time and my small-town journalism skills in an attempt to draw public attention to this case, with its roots in Berrien County, Michigan. In the process, inmate Floyd Caldwell had introduced me to inmate Maurice Carter who, he contended, had also been wrongly convicted in Berrien County. I had my hands full trying to work on the Caldwell case, so I wasn't about to take on another.

As hard as I tried, and as good as I thought I was, I simply couldn't seem to help "Sonny" Caldwell. His wife and I kept tripping over each other as she also worked for his freedom. We didn't see eye-to-eye on timing or methodology or much of anything. Our chemistry wasn't good. Tensions were high.

Of all the alleged incidents of injustice in Berrien County, the Caldwell case is perhaps cited the most. The Caldwell and Carter cases are mentioned by author Alex Kotlowitz in his insightful book, *The Other Side of the River*.

Both crimes occurred in the 1970s.

In the first, an elderly Berrien County judge and his wife were confronted by a man with a small knife as they parked their car in their garage. Reports vary about injuries, if there were any. It was a clear case of robbery. The perpetrator fled with some jewelry and a small amount of money.

I got the impression from speaking with Caldwell that he knew who committed the crime, but one of the victim's rings was traced to him, and he was arrested.

Now get this: Caldwell was found guilty in a nonjury trial and handed not one, but two life sentences: one for robbing the judge, and one for robbing the judge's wife. It was later learned that the sentencing judge was an acquaintance of the judge who had been robbed, although he denied this at the time of the trial.

A series of factors, including a less-than-perfect prison conduct record and the constant and sometimes dramatic efforts of Caldwell's wife to draw attention to his case—none of which have anything to do with innocence or guilt—did nothing to help his situation.

At last report, nearly all avenues of appeal had been exhausted, and Caldwell was still in the Michigan prison system serving time for a crime that almost certainly was committed by someone else.

I believed in his innocence and tried to help. My contacts in the media weren't as helpful as I had hoped. Our conversations would begin well, but as soon as I mentioned that I was trying to assist an African-American man who was in prison for life and who claimed innocence, discussions quickly ended. I would be dismissed with some sort of condescending statement like, "Good luck, Doug. We need people like you."

In the spring of 1997, during my travels as a church organ salesman, I met a minister's wife who was a legitimate handwriting analyst. In my usual impulsive style I explained that I was working with a couple of prisoners and wondered if she would analyze their handwriting for me. I explained that I needed to get my arsenal as full as possible if I were to fight for these guys. She agreed.

I quickly wrote a note to Caldwell and another to Carter requesting handwriting samples.

In no time, Caldwell called me up, chewed me out, and threw me away. He accused me of doubting his story. Maurice Carter, on the other hand, quickly returned a handwritten note and thanked me for trying to do something positive.

I later learned that Caldwell had taken Carter off into a corner when they were still living in the same facility. The message was in regard to Doug Tjapkes. "I don't want him any more. Will you take him?"

Now that'll do wonders for the ego!

The entire Caldwell ordeal had left such an unpleasant taste in my mouth that I was hesitant to do anything for Maurice Carter or anyone else behind bars.

I've paid my dues, Lord. I heard your challenge in the book of Matthew. I came to visit you when you were in prison. Now let me get back into the radio business.

I had spent nearly thirty years in the radio broadcasting industry prior to going into church organ sales in 1983, and I was determined to eventually go back. Radio was my first love. I believed that I was an expert in small-market radio; I knew that I was an above-average radio journalist in the small-market newsroom, and I was positive that God wanted to use me and my gifts to best advantage.

A few days after I mailed samples of the Carter penmanship to the analyst, I received an urgent telephone call at the organ store. It was the handwriting expert, and she wanted to meet me for lunch immediately. She would drive to Grand Rapids from her small community an hour away. We met at a food joint in a nearby mall. This time she wasn't all smiles, a docile minister's wife. She glared at me across the table and spat out the words, "This man did not commit that crime!"

Well, that's what I thought, but I wasn't going to spend the rest of my life trying to prove it, only to be embarrassed by another dismissal from another flustered inmate.

She grabbed my arm. "You've got to do something about this. Maurice Carter is not capable of committing a crime like attempted murder. He's a kind and gentle man. He doesn't belong in prison!"

So now we've got a problem here. You can put a label on it and call it a moral dilemma or you can pass it off as "mind games," but I can't just ignore this stuff. If I call myself a Christian, and if that means that I must strive to be Christ-like (the Lord knows I've never been a very good model of Christ-like behavior), then I cannot ignore Maurice Carter and his plight, despite our differences.

To say that Maurice Carter and Doug Tjapkes are different would be a gross understatement. Race was not our only difference. Maurice lived next door to a red-light house in a Gary, Indiana ghetto when he was a little boy. I lived in the upstairs apartment of a corner neighborhood grocery store in an all-white neighborhood of Muskegon, Michigan. He ran errands to and from a drycleaning establishment for women of the night for his spending change. I sold soda pop from an old-fashioned Coca Cola cooler filled with ice on the sidewalk next to our store. Maurice attended school with his black friends in the inner city but didn't finish his high school education until he was incarcerated. I attended private, Christian schools for my K-12 education.

I submit, however, that it's not all that unusual for me to pick up the cause of a falsely charged and wrongly convicted black man. Let's discuss my parents first.

My father, the only one of thirteen children of Dutch immigrants to go into private business, befriended an elderly black man who wanted produce scraps from the grocery store for his pigs. Before Mr. King died, he and my dad became best of friends, and I know that John Tjapkes made an extra effort to do nice things for Mr. King. I well remember the time that my mother baked a cake for Mr. King's birthday, and my mom and dad delivered it to him at his modest little farmhouse.

One year, instead of continuing a tradition of inviting family and friends to the annual Thanksgiving feast, my mother invited a rotund African-American woman with no legs who lived at the county poor farm to be the guest of honor. After the meal our guest sang an old gospel hymn in thanks. It was a holiday dinner that we never forgot.

My mom began her own personal ministry of writing to prisoners. I have no idea how that started, but I had private concerns that she was being exploited by con men behind bars. Looking back, I believe that her kind words touched lives.

As a child I was never allowed to walk the two blocks to a small half-block section of housing where African-American people lived. We were rather afraid of them. My exposure to persons of color really began at the age of seventeen when I took my first radio job. It was my duty to be the sign-on announcer at WMUS each Sunday morning, and the early morning programming featured live music by African-American singing groups. I became friends with the legendary show host Matty Davis, worked with the likes of the Heavenly Echoes, and promoted the singing of my favorite group, the Spiritualaires.

Years later, as a broadcast newsman in our mostly white community, I won the "Freedom of Justice" award from the State Bar of Michigan for my broadcast editorial criticizing the local newspaper for its unfair treatment of a black truck driver who had been falsely accused of raping a mentally challenged white woman. He was later freed and she was charged with filing a false report.

In the daily talk show that I hosted on local radio for many years, I would occasionally feature an itinerant black preacher named Sy Young who could recite most of Martin Luther King's speeches by heart. As our friendship deepened, he would share dreams of getting blacks and whites to work together. "Douglas," he would say in his booming Santa Claus voice, "when I get to heaven and God asks me if I had any white friends, I don't wanna say 'no.' I'm afraid he's going to stop me from going through the pearly gates!" Before he died from injuries suffered in a car-pedestrian accident, I often called on his considerable talents as a narrator for prison concerts.

My avocation was and is church music. As founding director of a male chorus called His Men, I promoted singing in jails and prisons during the 1970s and 1980s. Brother Sy, an entertainer before he met Christ, was completely at home hosting our popular all-white choir as it performed before predominantly black prison audiences.

That was the background and experience I brought with me to my encounter with Maurice Carter and my study of the circumstances that linked him with a 1973 shooting in Benton Harbor, Michigan.

It was beginning to look a lot like Christmas.

Gwen Jones (now Gwen Baird) was the only employee in the Harbor Wig and Record Shop in the downtown business district on December 20, 1973. A big, dark-skinned black man with whiskey on his breath was the only customer, and he wasn't the friendliest of sorts. Baird later told me she was convinced that this guy was going to hold her up, and so she was relieved when the little bell tinkled to signal the arrival of more customers.

Off-duty Benton Harbor police officer Tom Schadler and his wife entered the store and asked about a certain Elvis Presley tape. As she searched for the recording, Baird looked up to see the black man standing behind the white man and aiming his pistol at the man's head and neck. Several shots rang out, and Baird dropped to the floor behind the counter. Ruth Schadler screamed and tugged on the assailant. Amazingly, although he was struck by five or six of the .22 caliber bullets and bleeding profusely, Schadler was able to struggle on all fours to the front door, free up his weapon, and get off a couple of shots at the fleeing culprit.

Meanwhile, just a short block away in an old run-down hotel, Maurice Carter was being awakened by his friend, Wilbur Gillespie. "You gonna sleep all day?"

Carter had decided to visit Benton Harbor, thinking that the scene was getting just a little too rough and tough in Gary. It was time for him to check out another town. His timing could not have been worse.

Minutes later, as Carter stepped through the hotel doorway, a policeman confronted him, informing him that there had been a robbery down the street. Would he mind if the officer walked him past the store? Investigators wanted to know if the store clerk recognized Carter as the shooter. Having nothing to fear, he readily agreed. Maurice was paraded past the front window on the sidewalk. Baird insisted then, as she does now, that the guy with the gun bore no resemblance to the lighter skinned Maurice Carter. He was released.

No arrest was made for two years, which was not a good thing in a racially troubled area where a black man had shot and injured a white cop. This case needed closure. Fast forward to 1975, and tunnel-visioned police officers and prosecutors finally got their way. Their only suspect, Maurice Carter, was arrested.

I had spent most of my life covering news in western Michigan's Kent and Ottawa Counties where, I believed, the judicial system was doing a pretty good job. I thought the cops and prosecutors were the good guys, and the bad guys went to jail. That's what I reported day in and day out in my newscasts. I still believe in that concept some of the time.

But now as I reviewed the case records of Maurice Carter, I learned that his arrest warrant was based on a perjured affidavit signed by a jailhouse snitch two years after the crime, that he was paraded before the store clerk at the time of the crime and she had adamantly insisted that he was *not* the shooter, that he was identified in police lineups upon his arrest only after his picture appeared at the top of the front page of the local newspaper, and that he was convicted by an all-white jury skillfully manipulated by a prosecutor who had no physical evidence, no fingerprints, no weapon, and couldn't even establish a motive. He used only eyewitnesses to establish his case, even though some of the accounts were conflicting and the primary witness was an employee of the prosecutor (hired before the trial and "released" after the trial). What's more, the snitch recanted in the courtroom, and the state arrested him for lying about Maurice Carter. In other words, the State of Michigan actually *agreed* that what the snitch had said was a lie, but the trial continued anyway.

Upon conviction on a charge of assault with intent to murder, Maurice Carter was given a *life sentence*. With the sentencing guidelines of our state today he might get fourteen years. An attorney friend in Toronto told me the crime would draw about six years in Canada.

One didn't have to be all that acute to note that this case had an unpleasant odor. In fact, I would call it a stench. This indigent black man with almost no family and very few friends had fallen between the cracks. All indications were that he would never climb out, not without a boost.

The parole board insisted that he show remorse and confess to the crime if he ever hoped to get parole. That concept has always set my mind spinning. How could reasonable people come up with that? No innocent person with any integrity is going to show remorse for something he or she didn't do, let alone confess to the crime. What this tells me is that the scoundrels in our prisons who know how to push and pull the right buttons and switches can get out. The ones who have integrity and stick to their claims of innocence are rewarded by being allowed to rot in prison.

In the case of Maurice Carter, the cards were stacked much more firmly. The man who was shot and injured in the crime, police officer Tom Schadler, was later promoted to Chief Investigator for the Berrien County Prosecutor's office, and it is the job of the prosecutor to review each application for parole. A Carter parole had a snowball's chance in you-know-where.

There's more. During a part of Maurice's incarceration, the chair of the Michigan Parole Board was Steve Marschke, a former Berrien County Sheriff. Talk about a good ol' boy's club! This gang effectively saw to it that Maurice Carter would never gain freedom. I cannot imagine why they were so convinced of his guilt, without a shred of evidence to convict him.

Maurice once told me that, when the jury handed down the verdict in his case, the wheels of justice ground to a halt.

What kind of system is this?

By the time I received Maurice's telephone call in mid-1997, I had made the decision that he was innocent and needed help. He had been getting periodic and sporadic help from friends and supporters, but now he needed something constant, something consistent. I didn't see where I had much of a choice but to step up to the plate.

OK Lord, you win. But I'm counting on you for a lot of help. You saw what happened the last time I tried this!

Little did I realize where this relationship would go.

Little did I know what the prison doctors were already discussing back then.

I clicked on zero to signal that I would accept the charges. "Hey Maurice, how's it going?"

THREE

September 1998

Maurice Carter often teased me about making the painful decision to jump aboard. I accused him of leading me along like a mouse, throwing tiny bits of cheese, one at a time, until I walked right into the trap. He frequently reminded me of those little bits of cheese.

Strangely enough, once I made the decision to work with Maurice, there were no more doubts. My mind was made up and I dove in. I rolled up my sleeves. Maurice Carter's team had effectively doubled in size. He was no longer walking the path alone.

To say I was pissed would be to put it entirely too mildly. I was incensed! Was race the problem? Was the entire system corrupt in Berrien County? The documents I had studied revealed a kangaroo court scene. This was a story straight out of the old south. About the only difference, as Scott Elliott, the chair of the Citizens Committee for the Release of Maurice Carter, remarked some years later, "We don't have lynchings here. We have genteel lynchings. We bury them alive in prison."

My family stood by my decision. If Marcia or any of our kids or their spouses had doubts, they never voiced them in my presence. With my friends, it was a different story. Some of them didn't come around to my position for years. One of my good friends is Ottawa County Prosecutor Ron Frantz.

We have lunch together almost every Saturday noon, and he will agree that a polite skepticism hovered over our Maurice Carter discussions at first. But eventually *all* came around to my position, and Ron actually took on the role of confidant. He led me through complicated legal issues, all the while, I think, becoming more strongly convinced that we were on the right track. I wish every county in the land had such a conscientious Christian serving as its top attorney.

Well, as you might guess, the inevitable happened. It began so slowly and in such a subtle manner that I barely noticed it at first. I started liking this Maurice Carter. Always kind, gentle, and unassuming, he made no unfair demands of me, always demonstrated strong gratitude for everything I did, and took a genuine interest in my job, my wife, and my family. He never asked for money and never complained. Maurice appreciated my visits whenever they were possible and accepted my reasons for not visiting him when I couldn't. He never took advantage of the privilege of placing collect telephone calls and never made a pest of himself.

You didn't tell me that friendship—no, real love for one another—was going to factor into this equation!

In later years, Maurice said that this was the time in his life that a spark of faith in both God and man was being rekindled.

Enter the Innocence Project

DNA testing was giving many prisoners new hope. If any biological evidence had been collected at the scene of a crime, this method of testing could establish the identity of the person connected to the evidence. Thanks to a new organization called the Innocence Project, founded in New York by Barry Scheck and Peter Neufeld in 1992, wrongful convictions were being overturned by DNA testing. Innocent people were being set free.

The freeing of wrongly convicted prisoners did not go unnoticed by Maurice Carter. He insisted that we try to persuade Scheck to get involved in our case even though no
biological evidence was found at the scene of the Schadler
shooting. We kept trying. And, abiding by his policy of han-
dling only DNA cases, Scheck kept refusing.

Soon, however, a national phenomenon took hold. More
Innocence Projects were being created, most of them affili-
ated with university law schools. In 1997, the University of
Wisconsin-Madison Law School joined what was later to
become the Innocence Network. The Wisconsin Innocence
Project was cofounded and codirected by Professors Keith
Findley and John Pray.

On a Thursday evening in autumn 1998, after a particularly
discouraging period when I felt we were making absolutely
no progress, I accepted Maurice's collect telephone call. "Hey
man, guess what?"

I grumbled a reply.

"An Innocence Project is considering our case!"

"You're kidding me!"

"I'm serious, man! Barry Scheck contacted these people
running an Innocence Project at the University of Wisconsin.
Scheck said that he couldn't take our case because it didn't
qualify for DNA testing, but Wisconsin doesn't have that rule.
He told those guys that our case deserved their attention.
They want to review our material!"

Both Maurice and I pounced on Professor Findley and in-
undated him with letters, telephone calls, and documents. By
this time we worked together like a well oiled machine. We
weren't going to let this get away. Wisconsin took the case.

Lord, you are so good!

Professor Findley decided to personally head up the legal
effort, and he appointed one law student, Jennifer Anderson,
to assist him.

Findley's reaction to the documents was a familiar one. The more he got into the case, the more he became convinced that the trial was a sham and the defendant was indeed innocent. The more he became convinced of innocence, the more students he assigned to the project. This ball was rolling.

FOUR

MAY 1999

"Doug, when you and Reverend Hoksbergen go to Indiana on the fourteenth," Maurice had written in his last letter, "could you buy my mother a bouquet of flowers for me?"

Al Hoksbergen and I stared in disbelief as we drove down Broadway Street in Gary. This was another Benton Harbor, with its boarded-up houses and places of business, steel bars protecting the windows of liquor and pornography stores, and people aimlessly walking the streets. As we followed Maurice's directions to his mother's little house it seemed we were in an even worse neighborhood.

I had informed Maurice in our last telephone conversation that I would be his stand-in for Mother's Day. Al, our retired pastor, had also befriended Maurice, and so the two of us would drive to Gary just prior to Mother's Day, deliver some groceries and gifts, a flower, and a greeting card to Elizabeth Fowler. When we had visited in the past, her cupboard was always bare. She said more than once, "I was hoping you'd bring some food. I don't have anything to eat in this house!" I think we brought more food each time. Later I told a television reporter, "Maurice would have done this for me. I will do it for him."

Thus began a tradition.

Twice a year (just before Mother's Day and Christmas), Al and I would fill the car with goodies, stop to buy a flower or a plant, and aim for the home of Maurice's mom. There we would spend what today would be labeled "quality time" with this delightful and delighted octogenarian in her rundown little dwelling on Ohio Street. It was a ceremony that we hated and loved.

We hated it for what we could *not* accomplish, for not having an answer to a mother's entreaty, "When is my baby coming home? He didn't do anything wrong!"

We loved it for what we *could* accomplish: "Maurice sent this pretty flower to you!"

"He did? That Maurice, he never forget his mama. He was always a *good* boy!"

One year the Mother's Day visit attracted the interest of a Grand Rapids television station. A reporter and cameraman invaded the home of Mrs. Fowler with me, and she didn't mind in the least. Another year, a reporter from the *Gary Post-Tribune* brought her photographer along to do a Mother's Day feature.

I consented to media requests to eavesdrop on this intimate little visit on one condition: They must never show or say anything that would be an embarrassment to Maurice, his mom, or this family.

On occasion, Maurice would call while we were there, a special treat for his aging mom whose health was failing, and whose mind had a tendency to wander a bit.

"Is that my baby?"

Every year, Al would end our visit with a prayer, all of us standing in a circle in that overcooked, overcrowded living room holding hands.

Maurice would first hear about the visit from his excited mom ("Moms" he called her when he was polite; "Shorty" he called her when he was teasing), then he would extract every little detail from me in our next telephone conversation.

During our Gary visits, I would tell Mrs. Fowler that, since Maurice was my brother, she was *my* mother, too! That would make her laugh uproariously. When I related this story to Maurice, it would sometimes make both of us weep. "Thank you, Big Bro! (That was my nickname, forever and ever.) I love you for doing this for me."

Nothing else I have ever done, in observance of either of those holidays, has been more meaningful.

Lord, when did we see you hungry and feed you? [1]

1983

"In 1973, did you own a twenty-two caliber revolver?"

"No."

"Have you ever shot anyone in your life?"

"No."

"Were you and Wilbur Gillespie planning to rob the Harbor Wig Shop?"

"No."

"Did you shoot Office Schadler with a twenty-two caliber revolver?"

"No."

"Did you know for a fact who shot Officer Schadler?"

"No."

"At the time of the shooting, were you at the Benton Harbor Hotel?"

"Yes."

"Did you fire a shot at Ruth Schadler?"

"No."

"On December 20, 1973, did you shoot Officer Tom Schadler?"

"No."

"Are you lying to me in any way?"

"No."

The lie detector test was being administered to Michigan inmate number #145902 at Marquette Branch Prison, located in Michigan's Upper Peninsula. The polygrapher was Peter Perdomo, former Miami police officer and forensic examiner, now the owner of a private polygraph firm in Georgia. He had been hired to conduct the polygraph test of Maurice Carter by a new cable television news network called CNN.

Locked up for eight years on a charge of assault with intent to murder, Carter never once budged from his claim of innocence.

Scrambling to get viewers and ratings, CNN was inviting people to send in their suggestions for news documentary topics. Terry Kelly, one of the original heroes in the Maurice Carter saga, contacted Larry Woods, host of the CNN show called *Special Assignment*.

Kelly, a former nun turned journalist, was the editor of the *Michigan Citizen*, a weekly newspaper first based in Benton Harbor and in later years headquartered in Detroit. She had received a letter earlier in 1983 from a prisoner named Maurice Carter. When the *Citizen* printed the letter in its entirety, Benton Harbor Policed Sergeant Al Edwards called Kelly in a fit of anger. Later that day Edwards, who Maurice claimed was the detective who helped to engineer his arrest, had a heart attack and required hospitalization. Kelly later published a major feature on the Carter case.

Believing that the story had all the makings of a national documentary, she forwarded her findings to Woods.

After agreeing that the story had potential, CNN set out to hire the most objective polygraph operator the network could find. The Atlanta-based news operation found Peter Perdomo right there in Georgia. Still ahead was the formidable task of persuading the Michigan Department of Corrections to go along with this. These were the days when news cameras were still allowed in the prisons on special occasions.

Permission granted.

For maximum impact, a camera crew filmed the actual administration of the lie detector test. Both Perdomo and Carter explained, years later, that CNN was so nervous about the outcome that the producers of the show demanded some dry runs. Perdomo twice asked the same questions off camera with the lie detector wires connected to Carter's body. Twice he passed with flying colors. The show would go on.

Including commercials, the Maurice Carter case was given thirty minutes in prime time on national television. Maurice was the star of the show. Connected to the necessary electronic gear, he passed the lie detector test in three different phases on camera.

> *Oh, be careful little mouth, what you say,*
> *For the Father up above*
> *Is looking down in love,*
> *So be careful little mouth, what you say.* [2]

Many years later, when I became involved in the effort to exonerate Maurice, I learned that both Larry Woods and Peter Perdomo were convinced that Maurice was innocent.

In 1999 Larry Woods learned (thanks to our excellent media coverage) that the Wisconsin Innocence Project had agreed to take on the Carter case. He was so anxious to help that he flew at his own expense to Madison. It was there that I had an opportunity to brainstorm with him and the codirectors of the Innocence Project.

In 2002, Perdomo signed an affidavit for Carter's legal team, to be used as an exhibit for the brief that would be filed in court.

Said Perdomo in that affidavit: "As a former police officer, I take personal offense to those who are convicted for violence against police officers. Nonetheless, I left the prison convinced that Maurice Carter was telling the truth and was not involved in the shooting of Officer Schadler." [3]

The legal team was convinced, however, that Appellate Court Judge John T. Hammond never even read Perdomo's affidavit.

The 1983 CNN television documentary should have prompted outrage, especially in Michigan. Instead, there was only mild interest, and it was temporary. The Carter case was soon forgotten, and Maurice fell through the cracks again.

That was not the only time the Maurice Carter case made it to the national networks. In 1992 the CBS news show *48 Hours* did a segment on the problem of an inappropriate racial mix of jurors in American courtrooms, especially with African-Americans on trial. A substantial part of that national network broadcast was devoted to interviews with Maurice, his attorney, a black juror who claimed that she was improperly removed from the list, her former employer, and Judge Hammond.

On national television, Hammond expressed his opinion that you don't have the right to have people of a particular race on the jury. Instead, you have the right not to have anyone *excluded because of race* (which is exactly what happened to Maurice). Asked the CBS interviewer, "Then what's all the fuss about?"

Responded Judge Hammond, in a sarcastic voice: "The defendant wants out of prison."

It was a great segment, and again it should have generated outrage in Michigan. Still nothing happened.

January 2000

"There's one question I want to ask: Who says this man is innocent?"

The question came from a scowling African-American pastor whose skin was so dark that it was nearly blue. He was one of a couple dozen community leaders who had gathered on Wednesday evening, January 19, in the New Covenant Community Baptist Church of Benton Harbor. The meeting had been called by the Wisconsin Innocence Project team to explain to community and church leaders what was going on.

Representing the University of Wisconsin Law School: three attorneys and five law students. Representing the community, drifting in one-by-one long after the scheduled time to meet, were a few community leaders and some interested observers; and representing the churches, a substantial number of black pastors. We were meeting in the church of Pastor Rodney Gulley, and he served as host.

Even though this is a great story, I'm going to break here for a moment to tell you about Pastor Gulley, whose name gets added to my growing list of heroes. Gulley's father was murdered in Benton Harbor while on a construction job. The crime was never solved. Gulley's son was murdered. That crime was never solved. Rodney Gulley has repeatedly been the victim of police racial profiling. Yet he remains in the inner city, fighting in God's name for his people.

In discussing the Maurice Carter case, Gulley often recalled his response to the murder of his own son. "I don't want them to arrest the wrong guy just so they can close the case. That solves nothing."

Back to Gulley's church.

Keith Findley was standing up in front of the sanctuary with charts and graphs, attempting to explain the long-range goal of his team, which was to obtain a new trial for Maurice Carter.

The community knew about Maurice Carter, who had been sentenced in 1976, and the community knew that there was controversy surrounding the case. But Maurice was an outsider, from Gary, Indiana, who had been visiting Benton Harbor when the crime occurred. Frankly, it seemed that people there just weren't that interested in a case that didn't involve one of their own.

The question from the preacher with the booming voice abruptly brought the proceedings to a halt. People looked at one another. Findley stopped in mid-sentence.

The silence was broken by the pretty voice of a stately African-American woman in attendance. "*I* say he's innocent," she said, getting to her feet, "and I ought to know! I was the only witness to the crime. I was the clerk in the store where the shooting occurred!"

That broke the ice. No longer were white professors trying to convince black ministers that some visitor to their community was innocent of a crime. Gwen Baird, a local public school teacher, well known by the clergy as a devout woman, would not be speaking an untruth here in a public meeting.

In that magic moment, the atmosphere changed. Everything changed. The ministers and community leaders rallied around the attorneys and law students and offered to help. They posed for pictures for the newspaper and television

crews that were in attendance. Before the meeting disband-
ed, the ministers insisted that everyone join hands in a large
circle and offered a prayer on behalf of those seeking justice
for Maurice Carter. That was the first of many memorable
prayers offered by Pastor Gully on behalf of Maurice.

I couldn't wait to share this story with Marcia when I returned home, and with Maurice when he called. The long
drive home seemed to take only minutes this time.

The investigation of the Carter case was off and running!

It was a lead story for television news and a front page story
in newspapers the next day.

*You didn't stop working miracles when you left this earth, did
you?*

SEVEN

JANUARY–FEBRUARY 2000

It was the morning after, and I was still riding high.

I was at my desk in Grand Rapids at Westfield Organ Company, trying to focus on the church organ business. This was the work that provided groceries for our table. There would be time for Maurice Carter later.

The phone call was for me: "My name is Scott Elliott."

The name rang no bell with me. Certainly not an organ customer.

"I'm a businessman in Benton Harbor, and I'm reading and hearing about the meeting last night. I think it is imperative that you organize a citizens committee to help you in this endeavor. We could do a whole lot of groundwork for you and for the team from Wisconsin."

Good idea!

"I'm willing to chair the committee. I'll make some telephone calls and I'll get out the announcements."

Thus began the Citizens Committee for the Release of Maurice Carter, an unusual group of people that bridged all racial, social, and income barriers. The organizational meeting was held February 22, 2000, in a small downtown Benton Harbor restaurant.

"We just learned that Wilbur Gillespie is in town. He's willing to meet and talk with us! Rodney Gulley says we can use his church." Scott Elliott was breathlessly giving me this information on the telephone. It was just one month after the historic meeting at New Covenant Baptist. It sounded like another was about to happen.

"I'm on my way!" My car could practically drive itself to Benton Harbor.

Wilbur Gillespie is the guy who blew the whistle on Maurice. He was, supposedly, Maurice's friend. In fact, he was the person who woke him in the Benton Harbor hotel room on that fateful day, December 20, 1973.

Cops swarmed through downtown Benton Harbor after Schadler was shot and injured, and I imagine that if you were black and in that neighborhood, you were automatically a suspect. Remember, after the police walked Maurice past the window of the Harbor Wig and Record Shop, shop clerk Gwen Jones was emphatic in stating that Maurice was not the gunman. Not the right color. Not the right shape. Not the right size. *Definitely* not the shooter.

Two years later, however, that important information was ignored.

Gillespie was arrested in November 1975 on drug charges. Maurice Carter's life changed forever when Gillespie, in an effort to save his own hide, falsely fingered Maurice in the Schadler shooting.

It was our understanding in 2000 that Gillespie was living somewhere in Missouri. If he was in town, we certainly wanted to hear his side of the story!

I could hear sirens as I drove into the inner-city of Benton Harbor. Nothing unusual. Several police officers had surrounded a home across the street from Rodney's church, while one subject was being pursued. The foot chase seemed to end rather harmlessly, smelly smoke from a nearby bonfire permeated the area, and bored neighbors returned to their previous activities.

Pastor Gulley was late, and we waited outside the locked church building.

A well dressed Wilbur Gillespie drove up in an expensive vehicle. Whatever kind of activity he was involved in at that time (something that demanded at least two cell phones on his person, both constantly ringing) obviously was a financial success. He claimed his occupation involved the selling of clothing from the back of his SUV. I think that perhaps pigs fly in Missouri, also.

"I feel terrible about what happened to Maurice, because it's my fault."

"He can feel terrible all he wants," Maurice told me as I related the details later in a weekly telephone briefing. "He's a free man. I'm behind bars."

We had a tape player running, someone capturing the Gillespie scene on video tape, and an open speaker phone connected to Keith Findley's office at the University of Wisconsin's law school. We weren't about to miss a word of this momentous meeting.

Gillespie was thoroughly questioned by our little group of committee members in the church basement. Having hosted a radio talk show, I was no stranger to interviewing. But I was no more thorough than the rest of our group. Everyone had questions, and no stone was left unturned.

If it could be believed, Gillespie's tale was one of intrigue and corruption. And if rumors could be believed, Gillespie was here to make amends because his mother was furious. She and Maurice's mom were friends.

Gillespie's 1975 arrest was on heroin charges and, as you might imagine, it was not his first. This time, police officers said, he very well might face life in prison. That is, unless he was willing to deal. If Gillespie would sign a statement (already in the preparation stage by the police, he discovered) indicating that he heard shots fired and then saw Maurice Carter running from the record shop on December 20, 1973, there would be a deal. Gillespie contends that he turned down the offer several times. Carter was his friend, and he refused to tell a lie that would result in the arrest of his friend.

Gillespie said he was persuaded to change his mind by another prisoner in the Berrien County jail, a man he only remembered by the nickname "Red."

"Red told me I was crazy," said Gillespie. "He said that by signing the statement I could get both Maurice Carter and me out of trouble."

Gillespie urged Red to explain.

"You agree to sign the statement, and Maurice gets picked up. Your charges are dropped. Then, when you get called to the stand in the Carter trial, you tell the truth. You confess that the statement is a lie. The judge will declare a mistrial. You'll be free, and Maurice will be free!"

Gillespie said that the argument made sense at the time, especially since he was facing life in prison. But, he said, he failed to realize that he was playing hardball in the major leagues. What is it they say about the best laid plans?

The story played out pretty much as planned, at least at the very beginning.

In December 1975 Gillespie and police detectives worked out an 8-page statement that he signed. Based on this affidavit, the Berrien County Prosecutor's office issued a warrant for the arrest of Maurice Carter.

While police began their search for Carter, drug charges against Gillespie were dropped; he was paid $150 cash and given a bus ticket to Lansing. At least, that's what he says.

Carter was arrested in Gary, Indiana, just after the start of the New Year. Thinking there was some huge mixup, he readily waived extradition. He told his mother, "I'm going to Benton Harbor to get this mess straightened out. I'll be right home."

He never saw home again.

Upon his arrival in Berrien County, Carter's picture was taken and his photo appeared on the front page of the daily newspaper of Benton Harbor and St. Joseph. Gwen Baird spotted the photograph and was so alarmed she immediately notified the police that the suspect whose picture appeared in the paper was the wrong man, but they weren't about to listen to her. The authorities knew whom they suspected, knew whom they wanted, and whom they were going to put behind bars.

It's amazing what a picture on the front page can do. The following week, officer Tom Schadler and his wife both identified Maurice in a police lineup as the shooter, even though they had passed over his picture numerous times in the previous two years without a hint of recognition. The same held true for Nancy Butzbach, a woman who "conveniently" (and temporarily) became an employee of the Berrien County Prosecutor's office and whose dubious testimony helped convict Maurice. Gwen Baird was not invited to view the lineup.

2000

In a certain town there was a judge who neither feared God nor cared about men. And there was a widow in that town who kept coming to him with the plea, "Grant me justice against my adversary." For some time he refused. But finally he said to himself, "Even though I don't fear God or care about men, yet because this widow keeps bothering me, I will see that she gets justice, so that she won't eventually wear me out with her coming!"

—Luke 18: 2–5

You couldn't say that Maurice Carter was pushy. Well, yes you could. He just didn't act like the pusher, and if you were the "pushee" you didn't seem to notice it until it was too late. His gentle manner had a tendency to catch you off guard.

At this point in the story, enter two prominent people, who later became friends, treasured friends, to both Maurice and me: Alex Kotlowitz and Rubin "Hurricane" Carter.

Alex Kotlowitz is a Chicagoan and author of three books: *The Other Side of the River, There Are No Children Here,* and *Never a City So Real: A Walk in Chicago.*

The Other Side of the River, which was published in 1998, recounts the story of the mysterious death of a young black man in the twin cities: St. Joseph, the white and affluent community that lies on one side of the river, and Benton Harbor, the black and squalid community on the other side.

When I say that Maurice *insisted* that I try to reach this Alex Kotlowitz, I don't mean to imply he was petulant and demanding. But, in his own quiet, kind manner he continued to insist that I do everything possible to make contact with the author. Perhaps Kotlowitz would write another book. Perhaps he could do something else to help us. Perhaps. Perhaps.

Like the judge in the Bible who was badgered by a widow demanding justice, I finally gave in.

Maurice knew that Kotlowitz lived in Oak Park, Illinois. I took it from there.

I sent a letter to him at his home address, not knowing what to expect. What I certainly did not expect was a warm reply, instant recognition of the Maurice Carter name, and a follow-up conversation that led to a lunch date in Chicago. In the ensuing years Maurice and I cultivated close friendships with Alex, which would not have happened without Maurice's urging.

The second part of this story involves more "pressure from the prison."

The word from Carter to Tjapkes was that we should garner the support of Rubin "Hurricane" Carter and his Toronto-based organization, Association in Defence of the Wrongly Convicted.

How was I supposed to do this?

He didn't know. He just wanted it to happen.

I started with our main attorney, Keith Findley. Perhaps in his role as codirector of the Wisconsin Innocence Project he had either met the former prizefighter, who had twice been wrongly convicted, or he knew someone in the AIDWYC.

It turned out that Keith *had* met an attorney from AIDWYC at an Innocence Project conference and had mentioned our case to her, mainly because our defendant's last name was Carter, also. There were similarities in the two cases. He told me he would try to reach her again.

Days turned into weeks, and I heard nothing.

Finally I persuaded Keith to look up the name of that attorney and allow me to call her. He promptly responded with the name of a Toronto barrister, Cindy Wasser. I dialed her number, left word on her voicemail, and waited for her response.

Days turned into weeks, and I heard nothing.

Then, out of the blue, a call from Toronto, and a huge apology. "I never neglect telephone calls like this." The message had been lost.

Cindy cut to the chase and wanted case details immediately. Keith Findley shipped everything to her at once. I don't know how all of this happened, although I am certain that AIDWYC's wonderful and efficient executive assistant Win Wahrer had a hand in expediting the matter. Our case was endorsed by AIDWYC! One of the AIDWYC directors planned to come to Benton Harbor to hold a press conference and make the announcement. Then, as soon as his schedule would allow, Rubin "Hurricane" Carter would also come to Benton Harbor to call attention to the Maurice Carter case.

Who am I, Lord, that you are mindful of me?

Like Alex Kotlowitz, Rubin "Hurricane" Carter also became a dear friend. A few months later I served as his chauffeur on several occasions, and I had the rare opportunity to deliver him to the Thumb Correctional Facility in Lapeer, Michigan, where he enjoyed a face-to-face meeting with *Maurice* Carter!

Radio Days Return?

"That radio deal just won't go away, huh?" These were the words of Maurice Carter in a letter to me dated February 20, 2000.

No, the radio deal wouldn't go away. In fact, I wasn't about to let it go away. I was headed back into the radio broadcasting business, an industry that I never should have left in the first place.

If the owner insisted, I would purchase all three bankrupt radio stations in nearby Muskegon, Michigan. But I had my eye on one AM station in particular, WKBZ, the station whose broadcasts filled the memories of my childhood years.

This station had been one of the first on the air in Michigan and had the prize spot at the center of the AM dial: 850. It had been sadly abused over the years, shamefully neglected by owner after owner until it went belly up.

I would nurture this treasure back to health.

The highlight would be nostalgia programming that the listeners in Muskegon would love, fortified with insightful local news coverage and provocative editorials by the owner/host.

The studios were located less than two miles from our home. No more long drives to Grand Rapids, crowded highways and traffic jams, road rage, terrible weather, high blood pressure.

I had learned a few things from past mistakes, so I proceeded into this venture with caution.

I lined up the best legal assistance I could find for FCC matters in Washington, D.C. Next, I found the best corporate attorneys in western Michigan that money could buy. The head lawyer was not only one of the best in the business, but a fine Christian who identified with my wishes and dreams.

Obviously, this would take money. As I started placing telephone calls and arranging meetings, the money fell into my lap. An acquaintance from many years before had made it big in the telecommunications business. I contacted him to merely ask if we could do some business together. In a subsequent meeting he indicated that he had the financial wherewithal and would enjoy going into business with me.

We shared Christian beliefs, a desire to operate a Christian-based broadcast operation, and we were ready to move!

Jesus wants me for a sunbeam, To shine for him each day. [4]

I started working on personnel and programming. Details kept falling into place.

I found a wonderful radio newsman, (Now that's usually an oxymoron in this day and age!) with a great reputation, a good voice, and currently employed by one of the bigger stations in Grand Rapids. After just one breakfast meeting, he agreed to join our team.

Radio programming is very different from what it was twenty years ago. Much of it is syndicated, and I was learning that some very desirable programs were available for the Muskegon market.

A sunbeam, a sunbeam, I'll be a sunbeam for him. [4]

I began leaking information to my employer in Grand Rapids, bracing him for my eventual departure.

Negotiations with the owner of the three bankrupt companies went smoothly at first. Attorneys were assisting when and where they could, but much of this had to be handled personally in clandestine meetings in area restaurants. I thrived on the drama.

Some snags started to develop, but they were minor. Because of the huge debts owed by the bankrupt companies, prices were going to be inflated. Sensing that I needed some professional assistance, I retained the broker who had helped me sell my radio station back in 1982. This proved to be an unwise move. His presence and brusque style were not appreciated by the seller, and things started to sour.

Abruptly, and I mean in an instant, two of the radio stations were gone. It wasn't the end of the world, however, because WKBZ was still available. The previous owner of WKBZ was Grand Valley State University, a fine institution with head-quarters in our own county. The school had first dibs on the station if the current owner failed, so we immediately contacted GVSU to see if they would sell the station to us. I persuaded our state representative and one of Muskegon's prominent business leaders to join me in discussions with Grand Valley to give up the station. What would they possibly want with an AM station in Muskegon?

With nearly superhuman efforts, I was able to get a private audience with the university president. He loved my ideas, but shifted me off to his underlings.

The university reclaimed my radio station, my dream, and then, to my dismay, converted it to a National Public Radio affiliate. The door had not only been slammed in my face, it was locked! First, three radio stations. Now, none. Decision final. The community was denied a fine new commercial radio outlet and I was denied my dream to return to my former profession. There was no more wind in these sails.

You and I have to talk!

There must have been good reason for you to give me nearly thirty years of the finest radio broadcasting and radio journalism on-the-job training possible. I'm good, and you know that I was committed to serving you in this new station. You knew that I would dedicate the operation to you. There was not a selfish motive in this dream. I was going to be your sunbeam in an industry that desperately needs a Christian presence. What's the deal?

I can tell you this: I'm near retirement age. I'm not going to take another stab at getting into the broadcasting business. Never again! There's no way my emotions will ride on that roller coaster again! That's it. Finis!

Within the next year I would learn the real reasons for this 30-year course in news writing and public relations. I would even learn how my twenty years in organ sales and my avocation as a church musician would help me in my final and third career. I called it the third of my career trimesters.

NINE

2001

In the field of wrongful convictions, David Protess is a legend. A professor at Northwestern University's Medill School of Journalism, Protess teaches investigative journalism, legal affairs reporting, and media law and ethics. I had not personally met this freedom fighter, but I knew about him. His investigative reporting had contributed to the exoneration of seven prisoners in Illinois. In the past five years he and his students had helped to free three innocent men from death row, one of whom had come within two days of execution.

ABC News dubbed Protess their "Person of the Week." Chicago Mayor Richard Daley proclaimed a day in his honor. His list of awards and commendations would fill this page.

Protess is now the director of the Medill Innocence Project at Northwestern, bringing together journalism students, journalists, lawyers, and investigators. The focus is wrongful convictions. His organization works hand-in-hand with another highly regarded Northwestern organization being run by his colleague and coauthor Rob Warden, the law school's Center on Wrongful Convictions.

By this time Alex Kotlowitz had become a good friend of ours. He had been doing some teaching and lecturing at Northwestern University and, one day over lunch, he learned that Protess was searching for a new project to assign his journalism students for the upcoming semester.

Alex told the professor about his experiences with Maurice and me and about the Wisconsin Innocence Project's work on the Carter case. "Maybe Doug wouldn't mind having you get involved, as well," suggested Kotlowitz. "Let me give him a call."

Wouldn't mind?

In no time I was on my way to the Loop in downtown Chicago and a lunch meeting with Protess.

Students were assigned to work with the University of Wisconsin team, which proved to be a dream blend: journalism students and law students, using their unique tools and talents to reinvestigate this case.

And with Protess came two more powerful names in the business: Professor Lawrence Marshall, founder of the Center on Wrongful Convictions, and Rob Warden, Executive Director of the Center.

God moves in a mysterious way
His wonders to perform.[5]

By this time, Maurice Carter and I were family. That means that my wife, my kids, and my grandkids were Maurice's family, also.

Your people will be my people
And your God my God.
—Ruth 1:16

Maurice would call twice a week, on Thursday evenings and Saturday evenings. The prison calls were automatically terminated after fifteen minutes, but inmates were permitted to call again. We had an understanding that he would continue calling until we both agreed that we had covered everything. There were constant headaches with the prison phone system, its haphazard methods of blocking telephone calls, its shoddy telephone equipment in the prisons, and its billing procedures. I would panic when no call was received on a Thursday or Saturday because of our standing agreement. Repeated telephone calls to the carriers would turn up some senseless problem, and eventually Maurice and I would talk again. The telephone bills were incredibly high, but I wouldn't trade those precious moments for anything.

The first part of both Thursday and Saturday conversations was devoted to family issues. He knew the names of all four of our children, their spouses, and all the grandchildren. In fact, he lived through the births of several of the grandchildren. If any other family members were at our house when the call came from Maurice, they would speak with him, also. "That's my family!" he would exclaim.

Prison visits were nice, but not terribly important. Because of my busy schedule, and because my work on his behalf often took me to Benton Harbor, Madison, and Chicago—none of which was located next-door—we determined that business travel came first, prison visits second.

Mailing and photocopying documents cost money, so we established a program where I would send Maurice a money order monthly, usually in the amount of $100 and sometimes as much as $200. I tried to make this a routine transaction so that he would never have to ask for money. "Tried" is the key word here. Sometimes I failed, but he wasn't embarrassed to ask for it if necessary. We were brothers, and brothers can talk about anything.

I used the telephone conversations to boost Maurice's morale. I adopted an unwritten rule. I would make it a priority all week to save up a couple of very positive, and, if possible, exciting bits of news. I would save these to the final minutes of our telephone conversation. It was imperative for me to end these precious times of communication on a high. My job, as he described it, was to be his eyes, his ears, and his mouth. A part of my job, as I described it, was to keep his bobber up. After he had received a particularly exciting piece of information, he would laugh, the timbre of his voice would noticeably change, and he'd say, "I'm going to sleep *good* tonight!" We ended every conversation with "I love you."

I used the mail for the same reason and to the same advantage. Every day I would collect a stack of things that I knew he would want to see: e-mail messages, newspaper clippings, pictures of the family, a cartoon, and correspondence from the attorneys. A packet would go out every day. He could count on it. Occasionally when shopping at Walgreen's I would wander through the greeting card section and find a particularly meaningful card about friendship. I would quickly sign it and send it separately in the mail.

I later learned that, in order to enhance his mental health, he would "ration" the mail packets, opening only one at a time and saving, for example, one more to be opened at bedtime.

For Maurice's part, he did what he could. He sent handmade greeting cards for years until new prison mailing rules put a halt to the practice. He was a great artist, and the delightful cards were sent not only to me but also to Marcia, our kids and grandchildren.

Because of our close relationship and the heavy publicity, Maurice became as well known in West Michigan's Tri-Cities of Ferrysburg, Spring Lake, and Grand Haven, eighty miles from the scene of the crime, as he was in Michigan's Twin Cities of Benton Harbor and St. Joseph. The members of Ferrysburg Community Church adopted him as one of their own, praying for him on a regular basis. Director Sherry Merz would report that members of the Kids Choir included Maurice Carter in their prayer requests every week without fail. Our granddaughter Betsi Ingersoll encouraged her entire class at the Grand Haven Christian School to sign a letter to then-Governor John Engler asking that Maurice Carter be freed.

With all of this going on, our friendship evolved into something rich, deep, and intimate. I've never experienced anything quite like it. He called me the brother he never had. I did the same.

I believe that all of this contributed to the evolution of his personality. His incredible patience and kindness became legendary. His faith in God and mankind grew daily as we worked together, and I can honestly say that he became more Christ-like as time moved on. Prisoners noticed it, prison workers noticed it, and all who visited him noticed it. Law students and journalism students would leave the prison in tears. I know of no one who visited Maurice Carter who wasn't moved by the experience.

Our mutual friend Al Hoksbergen just couldn't get over Maurice's demeanor. "If they put me behind bars, and I knew that I was innocent I'd be a raging bull," said Al.

Not until long after I met Maurice, however, did I learn that his favorite hymn was "His Eye Is on the Sparrow."

> *Why should I feel discouraged,*
> *Why should the shadows come,*
> *Why should my heart be lonely, …*
> *His eye is on the sparrow,*
> *And I know he watches me.*[6]

Meanwhile, the case was moving along at a snail's pace. I did my best to push, but the legal team needed more time. Berrien County authorities were letting it be known that they were going to block our efforts every step of the way. As I tried to do everything possible to head off discouragement for Maurice, it became apparent that I was the impatient one.

Some days, our roles were reversed. He would calm me down, saying we were going to leave things in God's hands. "Every time we've had a delay, it has been for a good reason," he would point out to me.

Lord, give me patience. And I want it right now!

Hurricane Hits Shores of Lake Michigan

It was March, 2001, and former welterweight prize fighter Rubin "Hurricane" Carter looked like he was ready to take on the next guy to cross his path. He passed through the outer gates and into the lobby of the Thumb Correctional Facility in Lapeer, Michigan, a step or two ahead of his partner, Toronto attorney Paul Copeland. There was fire in his eye, and his quick step and wiry body belied his age.

Alarmed, I quickly walked over to him. "Rubin, what's the matter?"

He responded quickly, his voice booming with outrage: "That man didn't shoot *nobody!*"

Rubin Carter had just completed a visit with Maurice Carter, and I would suggest that the first Carter was a good judge of the character of the second. He had spent nearly twenty years of his life in prison on not one, but two, wrongful convictions. The 1999 movie *The Hurricane* starring Denzel Washington was based on Rubin's incredible life story.

As the Executive Director of AIDWYC, Rubin Carter had agreed to hold a press conference in Michigan on Maurice Carter's behalf. AIDWYC board member and attorney Paul Copeland had been in Benton Harbor to announce AIDWYC's endorsement earlier, but we wanted to milk this international support for all the publicity we could get. We wanted the Hurricane. And it worked magnificently for us.

The Citizens Committee for the Release of Maurice Carter had been planning the event for months. We made arrangements to use the finest hotel in St. Joseph as our headquarters. Rubin and out-of-town guests would stay there, and we would hold the press conference there.

The Wisconsin Innocence Project team members joined with citizens committee members to welcome "Hurricane" when he blew in on Sunday evening, March 11. What an experience! We sat around in the hotel bar until late at night eating, drinking, laughing, talking, and reviewing the Maurice Carter case. I finally went to my room, crawled into bed, and for the first time in my life spent the entire night in bed without one wink of sleep. Not one second. I was wired.

The press conference worked. Keith Findley used the event to announce the added support of the Medill Innocence Project, the Center on Wrongful Convictions, and the Michigan Innocence Project.

Behind every speaker in the press conference was a long row of chairs occupied by ministers, black and white, men and women. The Rev. Dr. Russell Baker of Benton Harbor's First Congregational Church, a member of our citizens committee, receives the credit for this near-miracle. More than twenty members of the clergy, *from both sides of the river*, signed a statement supporting a new trial. We later published the statement in a paid newspaper advertisement.

Rubin "Hurricane" Carter, playing the moment for all it was worth in front of the television cameras, asked, "Is there a special prosecutor's school out there that teaches them how to convict the innocent?" Warming up to his subject, he glared at the reporters and said, "Do you know what it means to incarcerate an innocent man? It is kidnapping, it is torture, and, in the case of capital punishment, it is murder!"

One of the reporters was a photogenic Dutch woman who lived in Great Barrington, Massachusetts. She represented a major television network in the Netherlands and also served as a staff writer for a Dutch magazine that I likened to our *Time* or *Newsweek*, *Vrij Nederland*. Her superiors had gotten a tip on the Maurice Carter case. She descended on Benton Harbor, accompanied by her television cameraman, with almost as much flamboyance as the Hurricane.

It's difficult to measure how much value there is in news coverage in another country, but we were proud to be rewarded with a 10-minute television feature in the Netherlands, as well as a major article in *Vrij Nederland*. Our case had moved beyond the boundaries of North America.

I'll not forget her account of visiting Rodney Gulley's church. She was obviously not a regular churchgoer, but she was impressed with the service and especially Pastor Gulley's message about wrongful convictions. Her final words to me in her Dutch dialect: "It vas a helluva sermon!"

Maurice told me later that the visit with Rubin Carter and Paul Copeland at the Thumb Correctional Facility (I was not allowed in there with "special guests") was one of the highlights of his life. Maurice hired the prison photographer to take pictures of them together, and, though slightly inferior due to poor lighting, those precious, grainy Polaroid shots were frequently used for publicity after that and remain treasures in our archives.

Rubin "Hurricane" Carter
and Maurice Carter

Déjà vu

Mid-day on October 20, 2001, gunshots echoed through the streets of downtown Benton Harbor. The sounds originated from the same street corner as the scene of the crime nearly thirty years earlier. Benton Harbor city police officers had the main street blocked off.

No crime was taking place this time, however. A leading ear and hearing expert from the University of Wisconsin was supervising some experiments with .22 and .38 caliber pistols.

It was the hope of our attorneys and law students of the Wisconsin Innocence Project to debunk the testimony of a key witness. Nancy Butzbach's words must have made a huge impact in the original trial, because jurors had asked to have a part of her testimony read to them again before finding Maurice Carter guilty of assault with intent to murder.

As mentioned earlier, one of the most unusual things about Nancy Butzbach's role is that she became an employee of the Berrien County Prosecutor's office shortly before the time of the trial. A short time after presenting her critical testimony in the trial and after the verdict was rendered, she was no longer employed by the prosecutor. Convenient?

Anyway, Butzbach testified that on the day of the crime she was working in the office of a private attorney, across the street and some distance away from the scene of the crime. She said that she heard the sound of gunshots, ran to the window of her office and saw Tom Schadler stumble out of the Harbor Wig and Record Shop and fire his gun. She said that she looked down the street to see what he was shooting at and saw a man running away from the shop. Later she told police, although the jury never heard this, that she saw the "shadow of a black man" running away from the shop. Is the shadow of a black man different from the shadow of a white man?

Our legal people felt the story was implausible for various reasons. Her office was nearly 200 feet away, it was on the second floor of an occupied office building where one would expect to hear typical office noises, the windows were closed because it was December, and there were outdoor noises because it was the Christmas shopping season—car and bus traffic, horns honking. How, they asked, could she possibly have heard the pops of a small .22 caliber pistol fired inside the little store? Remember, that door was closed, also.

Several of the law students and I were permitted to enter the office building (now vacant like so many other buildings in Benton Harbor), and occupy the very room where Butzbach claimed to have heard the gunshots. Our team worked with the police department ahead of time so that all area streets were closed (at midday on a Saturday … can you believe it?). Police officers fired the bullets into buckets of sand. Blanks could not be used, the experts claimed, because the sound is different.

First, the .22 was fired inside the former store. We *could* hear the shots, which really surprised me. Dr. Fred Wightman said later, in his written report, that was because we were not talking, there were no office sounds in our building, and there were no traffic sounds outside. Under normal circumstances at the time of the crime, he said, it would be "impossible."

The police later fired a .38 outside the store, and that was easily heard. If Butzbach heard shots fired, it was likely she heard the sounds of Schadler's .38, not the sounds of the assailant's .22.

Butzbach admitted in a later affidavit, obtained by one of David Protess's journalism students, that she knows guns, recognizes the differences in their sounds, and that she heard the sound of Schadler's .38. That discredits her earlier testimony that, after hearing gunshots, she ran to the window and saw Schadler tumble out of the building. It also discredits her testimony that she saw someone running away. The students and I reenacted that part of the crime. I shouted "bang, bang" from the front door of the store and a student ran down the sidewalk at full speed, proving that, by the time Ms. Butzbach heard shots and ran to the window, the assailant would have been out of her sight.

This type of work to build a new case for Maurice Carter took time. In fact, it resulted in delay after delay. The year 2001 passed and still our case hadn't been filed.

One of the many travesties of this case is that the judge never took a glance at all of this new evidence that took years to compile. If he had, he would have seen that the state never had a case against Maurice right from the beginning.

The year 2001 was a great one for the Citizens Committee for the Release of Maurice Carter. In addition to the visit and press conference by Rubin Carter, we organized a march on the Capitol in Lansing, Michigan, and we erected a billboard in downtown Benton Harbor. While the demonstration in Lansing was not very effective, the new billboard in Benton Harbor got noticed.

Somehow, some members of the committee were able to persuade a decisionmaker in City Hall to give us permission to erect a 12-by-20-foot billboard in a downtown city park. (We heard later that the guy got fired for this action.) The sign was particularly effective because it faced the scene of the crime. What a coup for our committee. The billboard was almost directly across the street from the building that housed the old wig and record shop, boasting bold black letters on white, with one of Maurice's old mug shots, also in black and white. "Free Maurice Carter," proclaimed the sign. "Justice now!"

Reaction was immediate and mixed.

News photographers, television camera crews, and even amateur photographers had a heyday.

The Benton Harbor power structure and business community were appalled. This was the type of news they had effectively kept under cover for decades. The last thing they wanted, as they tried to attract new business and industry, as they tried to change the image of their community, as they tried to depict it as a great place to live and work, was to hang out dirty laundry.

Billboard in Benton Harbor park erected by Citizens Committee

And this dirty laundry was seen by thousands. The sign was on Business Route 94 near a major thoroughfare. One newspaper account claimed that 6,000 cars passed the sign daily.

The citizens committee members were there for the unveiling, all wearing black-and-white T-shirts bearing the same words as the sign. Rob Warden drove to Benton Harbor from Northwestern for the October event.

"Berrien County courts and citizens must stop deluding themselves that wrongful convictions don't take place," said the outspoken Warden. "Of all the cases of wrongful conviction, nowhere is the evidence weaker than in the Maurice Carter case." The picture and article with quotes by Warden were on page one.

By the end of October our attorneys still were not prepared to file documents seeking a new trial. But one thing
was certain, thanks to the work of this little citizens group,
once the case *was* filed, all eyes would be on the court. Maurice Carter, at one time just another prisoner from Gary, Indiana with a name that no one recognized, was now becoming
a household word. Our goal to raise public awareness was
being achieved.

Even more important than the publicity was the impact
the sign made on the community. It led to our group's un-
covering a new witness and a brand new lead in the search to
find the man who really did shoot Tom Schadler, which you'll
learn more about shortly, in the next chapter.

Maurice Carter had been eligible for parole since 1986 but,
as I have explained earlier, the cards were stacked against him.
The man who had been shot in the 1973 crime, Tom Schadler,
later became chief investigator for the Berrien County Prosecutor's office, and it is the prosecutor who is contacted by the
parole board for input before making any decision. As if that
were not enough of a roadblock, for a time the chair of the
parole board was a former Berrien County Sheriff.

Maurice showed me a letter from a Berrien County Prosecutor dating back to 1986, when he first became eligible for
parole. Paul L. Maloney (who later became a Berrien County
Circuit Court Judge) strongly urged the Parole Board to deny
Maurice's application for parole, stating that Mr. and Mrs.
Schadler were the victims of an "appalling unprovoked attack"
in 1973. (No argument there, except Maurice didn't do it.)

The letter went on to say that "the life sentence imposed
on Mr. Carter was an appropriate sentence and should be carried out without modification or commutation. The crime
committed by Mr. Carter was a vicious and vile attempt to

kill another human being. It was a cold-blooded, premedi-
ated [sic] attack from the rear upon an off-duty police officer
and his wife. To release Mr. Carter after serving only 10-1/2
years of a life sentence would be an insult to the entire law
enforcement community, as well as a tremendous miscarriage
of justice."

Maloney also commented that "Mr. Carter has displayed
no remorse for his actions." [7]

In spite of all the obstacles, I must confess that I entertained
some feelings of hopefulness in May of 2001, when Maurice
was informed that his parole interview, which occurred every
five years, was coming up in June. Maurice had now spent
nearly twenty-six years behind bars, and he was a different
man from when he entered. The Michigan Department of
Corrections form advised him that he would be permitted to
have a representative of his choice attend the interview. Maurice dutifully returned the form well before the deadline and
made the necessary arrangements to have longtime friend and
Michigan Citizen editor Terry Kelly attend the interview with
him. Terry's home and office were in Detroit, only a short
distance away. A member of the citizens committee and one
of Maurice's earliest advocates, she was without question the
most knowledgeable about the Carter case and the Benton
Harbor setting. She was the perfect choice as Maurice's parole
interview partner.

On June 18, 2001, a sheet of paper was delivered to Maurice in his cell before the parole interview was even held.
Scribbled in longhand on the bottom was a terse message
from the Michigan Parole Board: No interest.

An attached sheet said, "Next Review Scheduled:
10/29/2006."

Maurice called me with the news. I had no response. Why
the heck couldn't they just meet with the guy and listen to
what he had to say?

Why, God? This is a child of yours. Nobody deserves treatment like this!

My life was no longer my own. True, I was still selling church organs and I was still on the music staff in my church, but the Maurice Carter project had become a full-time job. On Thursday, February 15, at the conclusion of a typically hectic day in early 2001, I wrote a piece called "It's Thursday." Following is an excerpt, and I stress that this was not an unusual day.

It's Thursday. I can turn off the alarm before it interrupts my senses with its annoying beeps. After a night of restless sleep and dreams of Maurice as a free man, I am fuzzily previewing my day, and not liking it. The shower will help focus the thoughts and stimulate the ideas. I start the day by offering the brief prayer of Jabez:
Lord, bless me; expand my boundaries; keep your hand on me; and keep me from evil! (I Chronicles 4:10, loosely translated).

A stack of e-mail messages that had to be dealt with last night before retiring were still on my mind: Maurice and I warned attorney Keith Findley not to meet with the Berrien County prosecutor and former prosecutor alone. They were not to be trusted. Rubin "Hurricane" Carter's secretary had a few questions. A new friend who heard me speak in a church wanted to send Maurice a money order.

Then, before going to bed, I put a brief announcement on the Maurice Carter e-mail Information Network. Some forty friends of our cause (the number would top 200 by the time he was freed) must be informed that a 2-part television series will be seen on the NBC affiliate in South Bend.

My first order of business after the shower is to grind some excellent coffee beans, start the coffee maker, and quickly grab that first cup as the water is still dripping through the grounds. The first jolt is important and jump-starts the thought processes. Then to the computer.

Attorney Keith Findley advises that he will be accompanied by students when he meets with prosecuting attorneys. He and I will plan to get together in Benton Harbor following that meeting. I will want to get as much information as possible for my Saturday evening conversation with Maurice.

Before heading to Grand Rapids I stop at church to put up a poster for an upcoming Maurice Carter benefit concert and place some fresh Maurice Carter newspaper clippings on the bulletin board.

My mind is not on the drive as I head toward my office in Grand Rapids. The ringing of my cell phone brings me back to the real world. Scott Elliott, our citizens committee chair, is getting close to winning the support of the CEO of Whirlpool Corporation, Benton Harbor's major employer. He needs my encouragement.

As I walk into the office, I find a pertinent *USA Today* clipping regarding the death penalty on my desk, placed there by a thoughtful colleague.

My telephone is already ringing. Joyce Gouwens of the citizens committee reports that one of the pastors is miffed that "Hurricane" Carter will not be meeting with them in Benton Harbor during his brief visit. I put her in touch with Pastor Gulley.

She also informs me that she has arranged for a speaker telephone for the next citizens committee meeting, which will mark the first anniversary of our group. Attorney Keith Findley will call us from Madison, at my request, to encourage the gang.

Joyce's call reminds me that I must issue a news release regarding that meeting. I write and fax it to more than two dozen media outlets, saving copies to be included with my daily packet to Maurice.

My cell phone rings. Tracey Tyler, legal affairs writer for the *Toronto Star*, is doing a big feature about Maurice and wants to get a photographer into the prison. Sorry, Michigan Department of Corrections won't allow it.

Fresh newspaper clippings arrive in the office mail.

Terry Kelly calls to ask for help in getting the Warden's permission to allow a visit between Rubin Carter and Maurice Carter. Our call is cut short. Scott Elliott is on the other line with another question.

I try to return to the organ business, but Professor Keith Findley calls to discuss publicity ideas. That reminds me to make a motel reservation in Madison, Wisconsin, because I'll be meeting with the Innocence Project team there next week.

As I begin the return drive home to Spring Lake the cell phone rings. Radio Station WSJM in St. Joseph would like a couple of sound bites.

By the time I check my home computer, there are seven new e-mail messages. Media. Committee members.

It's the evening for a call from Maurice, which comes prior to my church choir rehearsal. I can tell by his voice that he's down. The delay in filing for a new trial, while completely justified and done with his approval, has taken its toll. I assure him good things are happening. When I tell him how the journalism students plan to investigate the case, Maurice's voice takes on new enthusiasm. Then when I relay how one of the trial witnesses made a gaffe in her television interview, he yelps! Our back-and-forth banter takes on its familiar laughter and excitement. He received mail from two of the grandkids. The compassionless prison telephone timer clicks off our conversation before we pass along our regular "I love you" assurances. We'll pick up where we left off on Saturday evening. I race to church for the choir rehearsal. We include Maurice in our prayers.

At 9:30 p.m., Marcia and I finally belly up to the bar at Fricano's Pizza Tavern in Grand Haven, where our youngest son works one night a week. Having received an A on a speech about Maurice Carter just before he graduated from college, Matthew is anxious to hear the latest on the Carter progress.

Before going to bed I must send one e-mail message to our Michigan attorney, and another to the *Toronto Star*.

Totally, completely, and utterly exhausted, I pour a little brandy into a snifter to hurry up the sleeping process. I must remember to rent a car tomorrow for the Madison trip. I must make time tomorrow to drive to Benton Harbor ...

It was this kind of busyness that prompted me to make one of the most important decisions of my life. I think the decision had been coming for a long time, but I just kept pushing it aside.

For the past couple of years as our friendship deepened, Maurice shared with me his hope that one day he could convert all of this negative business into something positive. Upon his release from prison he wanted to help others who have been wrongly convicted. In later years, he even expanded on that concept and explained how he wanted to help all prisoners as they leave prison and try to put their lives back together again. He wanted to help them get jobs and pressed me to look into a program that he had read about called Second Chance. And he wanted to get involved in the process of persuading state officials to grant paroles and early releases to those prisoners who no longer belonged behind bars. He dreamed of starting our own Innocence Project, using students from the fine colleges and universities in western Michigan. The sky was the limit.

He loved to fantasize about those days when, once he was free, we would travel the country together to give lectures, sign books, and speak to students. I admit that I would not only keep the conversation going, but also sometimes even embellish these stories a little to pump him up. In reality, I had been giving little thought to that part of the future. I had my hands full dealing with the day-to-day battle of trying to get this man out of prison.

But, after one of those conversations in 2001, I gave it some serious thought. Why not? Indeed, why not get started now, before Maurice gets out?

John Carlyle, crusty corporate attorney who had been my counsel during my radio broadcasting days, had been reading about my involvement with Maurice Carter and was most complimentary. Even though he was semiretired, he readily agreed to my request for an appointment. I explained to him our idea of forming an organization that would provide advice and assistance to families and friends of the wrongly convicted, mainly using many of the methods that had proved effective in the Maurice Carter case. A tiny organization like I described certainly would not fulfill Maurice's grand dreams, but it would do something else that was very important. It would show him that we were on the same wavelength, and it offered him the prospect of employment upon his release.

Carlyle not only liked the idea but agreed to establish the organization as a Michigan nonprofit corporation and then undertake the much more time-consuming task of attaining

501c3 (tax exempt) status with the IRS. Another gift from God.

He did all the paperwork, and he personally paid any filing fees that were required. And, because the IRS had never heard of an operation like this, I swear that he nearly personally walked that application through all the hoops to gain approval.

It was another one of those stories that was so much fun to pass along to Maurice in our telephone conversations. Stories like this sustained him, renewed his fighting spirit, and allowed him to sleep at night with a smile on his face.

It was late in the year when we revealed the formation of INNOCENT!. Rob Warden used his opportunity in front of the media while dedicating the downtown Benton Harbor billboard to announce details of this new organization. Maurice Carter would serve as the executive director, even though he was behind bars. I wanted him to hold a position of importance like Rubin "Hurricane" Carter held with AIDWYC. It was my task to serve as the organization's chief operating officer, a fancy name for jack-of-all-trades. Someday Maurice and I would work side-by-side.

> *Let not your heart be troubled*
> *His tender word I hear,*
> *And resting on his goodness,*
> *I lose my doubts and fears,*
> *Tho' by the path he leadeth,*
> *But one step I may see;*
> *His eye is on the sparrow,*
> *And I know he watches me.* [6]

Rob Feenstra, the owner of Westfield Organ Company where I had been selling church organs for the past year, wasn't interested in losing me. He offered to allow me to work at both jobs in the same office space. I had two desks, two computers, two sets of telephones, two fax machines, two jobs! Rob permitted me to operate INNOCENT! out of my Westfield office rent-free. What a beautiful gift! We were off and running. Granted, we were operating on a shoestring, but we were off and running.

Now I'm starting to get the bigger picture, Lord! This background in journalism and public relations is invaluable!

MARCH 2003

"I was walking to the soup kitchen up the hill when I heard two shots fired."

As hard as I tried, I could not understand the words of Deven Williams, known to everybody in the 'hood as just plain Matty. Man this guy was a piece of work! Alcohol had done its damage over a period of time, to both his body and mind. He would laugh, talk, swear, choke, twitch, shake, kick, jump, slump to the point where I could understand nothing. He would be happy, then angry, then ask for money, then ask for booze.

My new friend Aaron McFee, who everyone called Dawg, stayed cool and remained the patient interpreter, feeding both his questions and mine to Matty as we tried to piece together the story.

"I turned around and saw Billy Lee running from the record store."

Matty was referring to Billy Lee Brown, the man who without question committed the crime that sent Maurice Carter to prison. I'll explain in short order how I am able to make this statement. But first let me continue here with Matty.

Dawg: "Tell Doug what Buddy said."

More gibberish.

Buddy, it turns out is really "Buddy, Jr." His father, also

nicknamed Buddy, was with Brown at the time of the crime, outside of the store while Billy Lee went inside.

"Buddy said that his dad and Billy Lee ran to Mama Nana's house on Meadow Avenue after the shooting."

No amount of pressure, persuasion, swearing, and shouting could pry any more information from Matty. He was finished. He wanted a ride back to the party store parking lot, and he wanted money. I was willing to give him a ride. Dawg pushed Matty into the rear seat of my car; he and I climbed into the front. It took just a few minutes to get to the party store where I slipped Matty a twenty as he jumped out of the car. He was ranting again, but again I couldn't understand a word. Dawg said he expected more money. He didn't get it.

I invited Dawg to stay riding with me as we drove to the scene of the crime. I asked him to show me where the soup kitchen was back in the 1970s, where Matty was probably walking when he heard the shots, and where Billy Lee and Buddy probably ran after leaving the scene of the crime. We then drove to Meadow Avenue, just a short distance from the old wig and record shop. Mama Nana's house has been razed since then, but Dawg showed me the corner where she had lived and where she had apparently hid Billy Lee Brown after the shooting.

I should back up and tell you a little bit about Dawg, and how our paths converged.

As Aaron McFee related the story to me in November 2002, he first read about us and the new trial in the local newspaper. He said to his mother, "If this Carter didn't shoot Officer Schadler, it's terrible that he has spent all of this time in prison."

"I have been in prison," he confided to me later. "No one should be there who doesn't deserve to be there!"

"That man didn't shoot Schadler. Uncle Billy Lee did it," Dawg's mother replied at the time.

"That's right. We all had to scrape our dollars together the next few days so that we could get Uncle Billy Lee moved out of here to Ohio."

"You gotta be kidding! Uncle Billy Lee shot Officer Schadler? What'd he do it for?"

"He hated white people, and he hated cops!"

Dawg said that he then told his mother she had to tell the truth and set this man free, and that's where she drew a firm line. She would do no such thing. "I love him like a brother," she said of Billy Lee Brown.

I was starting to get the picture. Blacks weren't necessarily going to help blacks in this situation. Maurice Carter was an outsider. He was a visitor in Benton Harbor, a resident of Gary, Indiana at the time of the crime. He wasn't part of the inner circle in the 'hood, and people in that circle had every intention of protecting their own. Carter could hang. No one would rat on their friend Billy Lee Brown!

This information simmered in the soul of McFee for a period of time, and finally he could stand it no longer. He had read that Pastor Gulley was a part of the citizens committee. He paid a visit to him at the church, using the alias Mark Johnson, saying that he passed the Maurice Carter billboard each day on his way to work, and now it was time to bare his soul. He told his story to a flabbergasted Pastor Gulley.

Gulley quickly dialed Madison, Wisconsin, and miracle of miracles, he got right through to Professor Findley. Pastor Gulley and the man identified at that time as Mark Johnson got on a speaker phone in Gulley's office, and as Archie McNally might say, "Keith Findley's flabber was just as gasted as Pastor Gulley's!" [8]

Keith quickly dictated his notes from that interview and fed it to all of us. I asked Keith to let me do some followup. Spring Lake is much nearer to Benton Harbor than Madison, Wisconsin is.

I must say that I grabbed that ball and did some pretty fancy running for an old man!

First I persuaded Rodney Gulley to get the guy in his office again so that I could interview him by speaker phone. He did, and I did. The mystery man told me essentially the same story that he had related to Pastor Gulley and Professor Findley.

Nothing happens quickly, especially when working eighty miles away by remote control, and trying to bridge a wide, wide gap between two cultures.

Through a frustratingly slow but nonetheless deliberate process, here's what happened:

First, we learned that our mystery man's name was Aaron McFee, and that he lived with his mother on London Avenue in Benton Harbor.

Second, some sort of rift occurred that turned McFee against Pastor Gulley. After that, he refused to work through Gulley any more. He went undercover. He couldn't be reached. For the moment, my pipeline was cut off.

Third, knowing I was effectively on hold, I finally persuaded a reluctant Rodney to give me the guy's telephone number. I believe Rodney felt a little chagrined to have been let out of the picture, but Maurice was my major concern.

Fourth, after a series of attempts, I was able to set up a face-to-face meeting with McFee in March, 2003. Our meeting spot: a Burger King restaurant in Benton Harbor.

When narrating the story firsthand, McFee explained that the Brown family and the McFee family had traveled to Michigan many years earlier from Arkansas. Technically, they are not related, but both families treat each other as relation. That's why Billy Lee is, to McFee, *Uncle* Billy Lee.

In addition to repeating the story one more time, he elaborated and explained that Billy Lee Brown, now living in Elyria,

Ohio, was a bully, a big, strong man who drank a lot and was a powerful fighter. McFee remembered seeing his uncle fight with other men. He also had guns, and he had access to guns.

He said that some other people knew the story, and that he felt he could arrange an interview with one of them. He refused to involve his mother, and at that time wouldn't even tell me her name. She didn't know he was an informant, and he wasn't about to tell her.

It was at that meeting that Dawg and I made an agreement to meet at the McFee home and interview Uncle Deven Williams, better known as Matty. And you already know how that turned out.

ELEVEN

2002

Studebakers brought out an adventuresome side of me that sometimes amused Maurice and at other times troubled him.

He was quite proud of the fact, for example, that back when he and I were just getting to know each other, my nephew Tom Kuiper and I flew to Spokane, Washington, to pick up a 1957 Studebaker truck. I had purchased it by telephone. The return trip would be on wheels. We drove that reliable little Transtar Deluxe through the mountains and the prairies all the way home! Maurice liked that story.

He was not as pleased about my drag racing ideas.

In addition to the truck, I own a 1963 GT Hawk. It's a rare Super Hawk, which means that it is powered by an Avanti, supercharged V8 engine. The Hawk is a big, heavy car, and certainly not the type of vehicle that one might expect to see in the annual Pure Stock Muscle Car Drags. But I had watched other, lighter Studebakers faring quite well at the drags as they competed with the more popular Pontiac GTOs, Ford Mustangs, Chevy Corvettes, and so forth.

We're dealing with one simple issue here: I love to race! I never raced legally before, but I owned fast Studebakers back in the days when they were making those wonderful cars in South Bend, Indiana, and I surprised a lot of guys driving well known fast cars. As a teenager, I drag raced my father's cars night after night in downtown Muskegon.

Even though the Hawk was too bulky and heavy to compete with 90 percent of the participants in the Pure Stock Drags, I was convinced it could make an impact. I worked with Art Vaandering, a fine local racing mechanic; twice we changed rear ends in the car to lower the gear ratio, and ultimately it broke fifteen seconds in the quarter mile, running slightly over ninety-three miles per hour; which is pretty impressive for such a big chunk of iron. Some fine new models today aren't topping those numbers.

Maurice loved to talk Studebakers, but he was a bit hesitant about the racing idea.

I took the car for some test runs down a drag strip in Osceola, Indiana, near the International Studebaker Meet. What a rush! I could race without worrying about the cops! I didn't race the fastest of all Studebakers, but I won seven out of seven the first time I ever drove on a dragstrip.

While speaking with Maurice in our regular Saturday evening telephone conference, he said, "Well, now that you've raced you can put the car away again. Every year you can get it out and drive it in some of the local parades."

1963 Studebaker GT "Super Hawk" on the track

He was gently suggesting that my racing days were over, and that I should now resume acting my age.

Was he wrong! And I told him so.

There was a moment of silence. Then he broke into raucous laughter. "That racing bug bit you good, didn't it Big Bro?"

It certainly did. I later claimed the dubious honor of entering the first Studebaker Hawk in the history of the Pure Stock Muscle Car Drags at the Mid-Michigan Motorplex near Stanton, Michigan.

Ezekiel went down in the middle of a field
He saw an angel working on a chariot wheel
Wasn't so particular about the chariot wheel
Just wanted to see how a chariot feel.[9]

Obituary

Tom Schadler died of natural causes in 2002, after serving for many years as Chief Investigator for the Berrien County Prosecutor's Office. This was a promotion he received after recovering from the 1973 shooting. Maurice Carter always insisted that Schadler was not qualified for the job. It was just one of a series of promotions and commendations that various officials received following Carter's conviction. Maurice went down. A number of others went up.

Prison Pastor

I became an ordained minister in 2002, which must have made my parents—by this time residing in heaven—shake their heads in amazement if not in amusement. I had started college in the autumn of 1954 as a pre-seminary student but barely lasted a year and a half. My ordination late in life came about because the Michigan Department of Corrections allows a private citizen to visit only one prisoner. In my new job as administrator of INNOCENT!, I wanted to call on other inmates. Michigan rules permit only attorneys and pastors to visit more than one prisoner and, as attorney John Carlyle put it so bluntly, "You sure as hell aren't going to become an attorney at your age!"

So, I became a pastor. It's not a very fancy license, and my only schooling was that famous institution of hard knocks; but my pastor—along with my friend Al Hoksbergen—put together a little ordination ceremony, we rented the main floor of a local restaurant overlooking the Grand River, and following the laying-on-of-hands we drank wine and enjoyed a meal together. There's no question in *my* mind that I am ordained of God to do this work.

The Forum

2002 was the year that the citizens committee, in cooperation with the Northwestern University Law School Center on Wrongful Convictions, presented a public forum on eyewitness identification at Andrews University in Berrien Springs. As with many of our programs, it wasn't well attended, but it was another great media event that brought in some big names from around the country. And it put our case once again on the front pages.

Council Resolution

Also in 2002, the Benton Harbor City Commission unanimously adopted a resolution urging a new trial for Maurice Carter, which was another major accomplishment for the citizens committee. Pretty impressive when you figure that this was the city where the crime actually took place and that Maurice Carter was *not* a native of this city.

Those were some of the important happenings in the year 2002, but the best was yet to come.

The Unoffical Visit

Maurice loved Keith Findley, but he insisted from day one that Keith underestimated the Berrien County judicial system. From the beginning Keith seemed to give Prosecutor James Cherry and his staff the benefit of the doubt and seemed to extend more courtesies to that office than were necessary. That annoyed Maurice.

A good example of this came in the Autumn of 2002, when our case was finally ready for filing. Keith opted to set up a meeting with the Berrien County Prosecutor's office prior to the filing to show them our documents. It was a long shot, but he planned to show Prosecutor Jim Cherry and Assistant Prosecutor Beth Wild all of the reasons why a new trial was certainly in order, and then ask them to abandon their plans and in unity give this wrongly convicted man his day in court.

Keith Findley (Wisconsin Innocence Project) with Maurice

In retrospect, we might have had a better chance at convert-
ing the Pope to Protestantism.

Cherry and Wild were firm in their position. They stated
then and in the media later that we had nothing new, and they
personally gave us fair warning that they would block our
attempt every step of the way, both procedurally and legally.
Our team chose to ignore Wild's insult that we purposely
waited for Tom Schadler to die before filing our brief.

Our folks left with tails between their legs.

Maurice said, "I told you so!"

Actually, Maurice had started on some of these issues quite
a bit earlier. Knowing that we would be going to court before
the end of the year he continued to raise issues that prompted
considerable discussion among himself, the Wisconsin legal
team, our Michigan attorney Gary Giguere Jr., and me. These
issues prompted discussion in the citizens committee meetings, also. Members of the citizens committee and Maurice all
insisted that justice could not be achieved in Berrien County,
that we should ask to have the case heard in another county.

Giguere, who had a track record of trying cases in southwestern Michigan counties including this one, was of the
opinion that we would gain little if anything by changing
counties. He predicted that if the court granted us a change,
we would go to neighboring Cass County. Of the two, said
Giguere, he preferred Berrien County.

Maurice held firm to his conviction that we should move,
despite all of the arguments. The other members of our legal
team who were in Wisconsin and Illinois seemed to think that
if the documents carried enough ammunition, right would
win … even in Berrien County. We learned, too late, that
Maurice and the citizens committee members were right.

The second point of discussion was the judge. The judge
who tried Maurice Carter's case was obviously no longer on

the bench, but the successor who was in line to hear the Carter case this time was Judge John T. Hammond. A debate ensued among our team regarding whether we should file for a motion for the judge to recuse himself. There was never a consensus. Even I was ambivalent.

But Maurice held firm once again. He didn't want the guy. He recalled when Judge Hammond presided over a Carter pretrial hearing in 1993. His attorney had asked the court to give Maurice a copy of the preliminary examination transcript at no charge and was interrupted by Judge Hammond: "You can quit right there! Counsel is something else, but if the defendant wants reading matter in jail, buy him an Agatha Christie. These transcripts are expensive, hundreds of dollars in these things. They are not toilet paper to be passed around … additional copy for him, absolutely not! As far as I am concerned, if you can talk a circuit judge into it, go right ahead. I am not going to waste the taxpayers' money for that. If you want to get a cheap murder mystery, you can get one for 25 cents."

The decisions that were reached regarding which court and which judge disappointed Maurice, but nothing could diminish our excitement and anticipation.

The Filing
It was cold and gray when I left home. I was suffering with a miserable cold and pleased to note that at least it wasn't snowing. The weather remained decent until I exited I-196 onto I-94 in Benton Township. Suddenly the wind, the rain, the sleet, the snow all buffeted my car in one big blast. Welcome to Berrien County. The weatherman must have sensed that another Maurice Carter event was in the offing.

This was our big day: Friday, November 22, 2002. Our legal team would appear in person to file documents seeking a

new trial. I cannot describe our feelings. This marked the cul-
mination of four years of efforts by attorneys, law students,
journalism students, and just plain citizens. Think of it: thousands of hours spent digging up new evidence, finding new
witnesses, sifting through police reports and court documents,
interviewing, brainstorming, realizing as the days and weeks
and months and years went by that everything pointed to the
wrongful conviction of an innocent man. Now, how to correct this shameful injustice? Certainly the judicial system that
we have respected in the past would not fail Maurice Carter
again, when presented with the full story.

By the time the legal team arrived on that November
morning, our Michigan weather was at its worst. The mer-
cury hovered at the freezing point, so the precipitation would
vary from snow to sleet to just plain cold rain—all of it coming at us horizontally because of a strong nor'wester blowing
in off Lake Michigan. It could not have been more miserable,
yet our spirits could not have been higher. We believed that
Maurice was on the way to freedom.

Professors Keith Findley and John Pray along with the law
students arrived late because of heavy Chicago traffic and the
rotten weather. They knew that we had a reception and press
conference planned for them in a fine public meeting place
near the courthouse. What they didn't know is what else we
had planned for them, and if the strong winds off Lake Michigan didn't blow them off their feet, this nearly did.

You can well imagine that we pushed our media and public
relations skills to the *n*th degree this time. By now reporters
had learned to trust me. They knew that when I sent out a
news release or media advisory by fax, it wasn't fluff. I had
finally established my credentials as a newsman. I had about
twenty on the media fax list then, and when the transmission
was made you could anticipate some excellent results. The
media did not disappoint us on this, the big day.

As the legal gang rounded the corner onto Port Street, leaning into the sleet and wind, they stopped in amazement. There, across the street on the sidewalk along the edge of the courthouse, was a crowd of some fifty Maurice Carter supporters marching in the unpleasant elements, singing and chanting, "Free Maurice Carter." The demonstrators ranged in age from tiny kids to senior citizens. Many were waving signs and placards which they held up so that workers in the

Demonstration outside Berrien County
Courthouse, November 22, 2002

prosecutor's office and the Circuit Court office could read the messages. Before proceeding to the courthouse, the Wisconsin crew quickly recovered and grabbed their cameras, furiously snapping pictures. They had never seen anything like it. Neither had any of the occupants of the Berrien County Courthouse.

And then came one of those spontaneous, once-in-a-lifetime moments never to be forgotten: Over the sounds of passing cars and trucks on the busy street just a few feet away,

Pastor Rodney Gulley called for silence and then in his strong voice offered a public prayer seeking justice. Tears streamed down my face. How could God resist this plea? How could I accurately relate all of this to Maurice?

Later, by the warmth of a fire in the fancy Priscilla U. Byrns Heritage Center, we provided the marchers with refreshments, hot coffee, and a place to dry out. Keith Findley held a press conference, calling this Maurice Carter's "last, best hope" for freedom. He took time to explain that there were no more avenues. All others had been exhausted.

How I wished that Maurice could be there, just to feel the degree of love and support. People had come not only from Berrien County, but also from Detroit, Gary, Indiana, and from my own community and church. They loved this guy, and many didn't even know him.

Findley pointed out what had become so obvious to all of us working on the case: This terrible injustice was brought about by mistaken eyewitness testimony and the testimony of a jailhouse snitch, two of the most common ingredients in wrongful convictions.

Prosecutor Cherry wasn't amused, and if he was impressed, he wasn't letting on. "I will not be pressured by public opinion," one newspaper quoted him as saying. "We're going to call this as we see it." That's what we were afraid of.

> *We shall overcome*
> *We shall overcome*
> *We shall overcome some day*
> *Oh, deep in my heart*
> *I do believe*
> *We shall overcome*
> *Some day.* [10]

One minor part of the demonstration failed miserably.

Some of us on the committee had wanted to make this event sort of a candlelight vigil, even though it was taking place late morning. It's difficult to see lighted candles in the daytime. Anyway, Michigan's November winds would snuff out flames on a candle in a heartbeat. So, we found some very inexpensive fake candles ... a little light bulb shaped like a flame on the top, and space for a battery in the tube beneath it. I mean, *really* inexpensive! I had boxes of those flimsy candles in my car as I drove to St. Joseph.

When I arrived at our headquarters near the courthouse, we hurriedly stuffed batteries into the make-believe candles. Some of the units broke, some refused to work.

The light on these little devils was activated by screwing the bulb in tighter, but there was so little tolerance between the contact and the battery that it was virtually impossible to turn off some of them. I drove to the courthouse with dozens of candle bulbs blinking annoyingly in the seat next to me.

> *This little light of mine, I'm gonna let it shine*
> *Let it shine, Let it shine, Let it shine.*[11]

The idea was a good, but the project was a failure. In broad daylight there was no way to tell whether the chintzy bulbs were lit or dark, on or off. It made no difference. The public and the media certainly had no idea that we were carrying candles, trying to make a serious statement. I don't think they even saw them. I believe we made a serious statement that day, but the candles helped not a lick! After the march, we dumped them.

> *Hide it under a bushel? No! I'm gonna let it shine,*
> *Let it shine, Let it shine, Let it shine.*[11]

It was the publicity from this single event that pricked the conscience of a young Benton Harbor Gulf War veteran nicknamed Dawg, who knew who had really shot Tom Schadler; and it prodded him to visit a pastor whose name was connected to the citizens committee.

TWELVE

2003

Some say his first and last names should be reversed. His name is James Jesse; he's now an elderly attorney who still works out of his office in Buchanan, Michigan. He was the court-appointed attorney who represented Maurice Carter in his first trial.

James Jesse's reputation was widely known. He served Berrien County for years as court-appointed counsel for many indigent defendants. According to numerous accounts, his inadequate defense resulted in the incarceration of a lot of people. Maurice never forgave him for the terrible work he did on his case. Even though he was not a vindictive person, he expressed the wish that someday a civil suit could be filed against the man who allowed the state to slam the prison doors on Maurice Carter.

Jesse failed to introduce and/or call attention to important information, he failed to question witnesses properly, he simply failed to do the job he was paid to do. Granted, he wasn't paid much, but that's beside the point. After he was convicted, Maurice filed an appeal and begged the judge to give him a different attorney, claiming that Jesse was a major reason for the verdict.

The judge denied Maurice's request and assigned Jesse to the appeal. To top it off, Jesse had to pay a penalty because he filed late. Is it any wonder that Maurice Carter had no use for James Jesse?

The word around the courthouse was that the court-appointed counsel could be seen falling asleep during court proceedings.

His license had been suspended twice. In 1993 the state lifted his license for improperly doing his job in nine different cases. The list reads like this: "failed to timely notice post-conviction motions for hearing in four cases; failed to obtain his client's consent to dismiss the appeal in one case; failed to file a motion seeking to withdraw in one case; failed to timely respond to the prosecutor's application for leave to appeal in one case; and, failed to keep his client's [sic] adequately informed concerning the status of their appeals in three cases."[12] And the list goes on. Yet, after only thirty-five days on the sidelines they turned him loose on the public once again!

History shows that Jesse just couldn't change his ways. In 2000 his license was suspended again, this time for forty-five days. Does this sound familiar? "… failed to notice trial court motions for hearing; failed to file an appeal or take any court action on his client's behalf; never filed a motion to withdraw from his client's representation; failed to maintain reasonable communications with his client; and failed to cooperate with the Attorney Grievance Commission in its investigation." [13] But, forty-five days later he was once again free to subject indigent clients to his ineptitude.

I got my belly full and raced to the Attorney Grievance Commission in 2003 to file my own complaint against Jesse. Here's what triggered my anger: An inmate in the prison system began contacting us around the first of the year. Also from Berrien County, the man had a checkered past, physical and emotional problems, and his credibility was questionable. First he contacted Scott Elliott, chair of the citizens committee. Then he spoke with Keith Findley, Maurice's head attorney. I had several interviews with the man, on the telephone and in person. I drove literally to the bottom and top of Michigan, Jackson to the south and Munising to the north, to speak with him in correctional facilities. I was on a mission. This guy may have had his share of problems, but it was my contention that he had something on James Jesse that was irrefutable. And, on Maurice's behalf, I was going to do my best to put that incompetent attorney out of business.

Our informer's claim was this: James Jesse, who had a relationship both as a family friend and a former attorney for the inmate, was now trying to persuade him to claim that Maurice Carter had confessed the Schadler shooting to him! That's right: Paid by the taxpayers to represent Maurice Carter, he solicited false testimony against him. He was successful in persuading the inmate to make that claim in writing. That document, we learned later, was in the hands of the Berrien County Prosecutor and would be used as another tool to oppose a new trial. What Jesse hadn't counted on was that the informer's conscience got the best of him. He has his problems, but he's a Christian, and he knew that he wronged a brother. That's when he started calling us. He wanted to make certain that we all understood that he wrote it under pressure, and that it was a lie. He further contended that members of the Berrien County Prosecutor's Office were also involved in this chicanery. We were never able to prove that, but we believed it.

After months of telephone calls and prison visits, we were finally able to get a handwritten affidavit from the inmate stating that James Jesse coerced him into saying that Maurice Carter had confessed the Schadler shooting to him while the two inmates were in the same prison facility in Muskegon, Michigan.

I checked with Maurice. He had never met the guy, and he gave me a signed affidavit swearing to that fact. In his affidavit, the inmate also swore that, even though the two men were in the same facility at one time, he had never met Maurice Carter.

I had the stuff, and I was going after James Jesse! I think you'll find in every state's judicial code of ethics that an attorney may *never* take any negative action against a person who was once a client. Yet, because we were claiming ineffective counsel as a major reason for a new trial for Maurice Carter, James Jesse was apparently going to do what he could to help the state keep Maurice in prison!

Since I was Maurice's eyes, ears, and mouthpiece, I was going after the man who caused him so much trouble.

The grievance was filed with the State of Michigan's Attorney Grievance Commission in July, 2003.

More than a year later, I had to inform Maurice that the Commission dismissed my request for investigation, which came as no surprise to Maurice. As small consolation, the Commission slapped Jesse's hand: "the Commission wishes to caution you regarding an attorney's obligation to carefully review all rules of professional conduct, court rules, and statutes relevant to a conflict of interest analysis before and periodically after undertaking a representation. The Commission is confident that you share its concerns in this regard."[14]

The Berrien County Prosecutor's Office held true to its word. Our documents asking for a new trial were filed in November, 2002, and the prosecutor's office resisted. Despite that, Judge Hammond handed down an order, in January 2003, giving the prosecutor sixty days to respond to our allegations and claims. We were mildly encouraged by that, and the judge's decision got some pretty good press.

Then began a series of maddening delays. As each deadline neared, the prosecutor's office would seek another extension.

Keith Findley, always the nice guy and hoping not to ruffle
feathers, reluctantly agreed. The longer the delay, the louder
the grumbles and complaints from citizens committee members and Carter supporters. It felt like we were being held
hostage.

Carter friend Lisa Connell and I finally took things into
our own hands. Scraping up dollars from here and there,
working with an advertising agency in Kalamazoo, we signed
a contract for another billboard in Benton Harbor. The location didn't seem to be the best, but in the long run it turned
out to be great.

On a rainy May 15, 2003, in brief ceremonies at the west
city limits of Benton Harbor on Business Route I-94, a new
bright red commercial billboard was unveiled. The big, bold
words shouted: "New trial for Maurice Carter **NOW!** Justice delayed is justice denied."

Citizens Committee members gather for unveiling of I-94 billboard on May 15, 2003

The media were be-
ginning to like us a lot.
Our news stories add-
ed some color to the
otherwise bland diet
of government meet-
ings, shootings, fires,
and traffic accidents.
The billboard made the
news from Grand Ha-
ven to South Bend. The
prosecutor's office dis-
covered that we had not
rolled over and played
dead. To the chagrin of

the power structure in the community, this little band of pro-
testors now had two billboards within the Benton Harbor
city limits attracting attention to the injustice of the Maurice
Carter case.

Assistant Prosecutor Wild filed her documents refuting our
claims on June 6. Said *Grand Rapids Press* editorial writer Ed
Golder: "Prosecutor Cherry's decision to stand by the verdict indicates more stubbornness than sense. There is ample
documentation that the conviction was at the very least questionable. Worse, it may have been wrong. The real assailant
may have gone free while an innocent man has languished
for nearly three decades behind bars … . Berrien County
may well have a compelling case against Carter, as Mr. Cherry
believes. In that case, it should have no problem convincing
another jury of his guilt. If such evidence is lacking, why is
Carter still in jail?" [15]

Why, indeed.

In April, 2003, I spotted an interesting feature in *The Grand
Rapids Press*. Staff writer Pat Shellenbarger wrote about his
service on a jury in Kent County Circuit Court. The jury
found the defendant guilty based primarily on eyewitness accounts. The point of the feature was that this reporter had
revisited the case later, met with members of the defendant's
family who still claimed that the subject was wrongly convicted, and at the end concluded that he still believed that he
and the jury were correct with the guilty verdict.

Knowing nothing about the case, I was in no position to
take a stand on innocence or guilt. I took a moment to write
a letter to Shellenbarger to explain the high percentage of
errors in eyewitness trial testimony (over 80 percent). He was
kind enough to get back to me, and inquisitive enough to ask,
"What the heck is INNOCENT!?"

He drove to my office on April 23. He admits that he was quite skeptical on the issue of Maurice Carter's innocence, but he was more than a little intrigued by my relationship with this inmate. We sparred verbally for a little bit, getting to know each other. By this time my friendship with Maurice had drawn the attention of numerous journalists. Steve Mills of the *Chicago Tribune* was toying with writing a cover story for the paper's Sunday magazine. Author Alex Kotlowitz was wondering where to go with the story, perhaps public radio, perhaps the *New Yorker*.

Anyway, Pat persuaded his editors to run with the story, but it wasn't a quick decision. First, he personally visited attorney Gary Giguere in Kalamazoo, Scott Elliott and Gwen Baird in Benton Harbor, James Jesse in Buchanan, retired police chief Al Edwards, and Maurice Carter in the Thumb Correctional Facility. He also had a telephone interview with Keith Findley. This guy was thorough.

On Sunday, June 1, 2003, there appeared a front page feature in *The Grand Rapids Press* entitled "Brothers In Law." The subheading: "A man convicted of shooting a cop six times finds an unlikely ally in a church organ salesman. Their goal: proving that the imprisoned man had nothing to do with the crime." Maurice and I were on the front page in full color, with our arms around each other.

This was perhaps one of the finest journalistic efforts on our behalf. We requested and received permission to make reprints for distribution far and wide. It was Maurice's favorite piece. Countless numbers of copies were sent to him in prison, a few at a time so as not to raise eyebrows. He enjoyed mailing the reprints to friends and family members.

By the time he wrote this feature, Pat now admits that he was convinced of Maurice Carter's innocence.

June 9, 2003. A huge editorial appeared in *The Grand Rap-*

ids Press, running from top to bottom of the op-ed page, entitled "Maurice Carter: Let him go."

Yes!

The feature and the editorial didn't go unnoticed. As the name Maurice Carter was becoming recognized, people were keeping an eye on the judicial system to see where all of this was heading. But there was a negative side: The judicial system became entrenched, determined to stop this case from heading anywhere.

Pat Shellenbarger and I became good friends. He was professional enough to realize that as a journalist he had to remain objective, but he and others at the *Press* wrote several more stories, editorials, and columns about the Carter case. Pat and I teamed up to do some investigative work in the inner city of Benton Harbor that resulted in a fine exposé, written by Pat, which should have led to an arrest of the Tom Schadler assailant and the freedom of Maurice Carter. And should have led to a journalism award for Pat. Note the words "should have."

Dawg was a friend. Maurice wasn't convinced that he should be, and constantly urged me to proceed with caution. In all fairness, Maurice was very concerned about my well-being. He just hated the thought that this white boy was prowling around in the black inner city. Maurice had lived in an environment where con artists flourished in their trade. He didn't want anyone to con me. I loved him for it.

I must say, however, that I have never felt that Dawg lied to me or misled me in any way. I didn't say he was always cooperative. He wasn't always reliable. He seldom was punctual. That didn't matter. He just couldn't be persuaded to work all the way with us to solve the crime.

He insisted that his family and many in the neighborhood

knew that Billy Lee Brown had shot Tom Schadler, but he wouldn't let me or anyone else talk to his mother. He went to the opposite extreme, and for months didn't reveal to his mother that he was talking with me. They had no answering machine or voice mail, but the telephone had caller ID. Dawg would check the list of recent telephone calls. Then, if his mother wasn't home and if he felt like it, he would return my call.

I mentioned earlier that he was a Gulf War veteran, and he was proud of it. He was also bitter that a guy who fought for his country still couldn't get a job in his own town upon his return.

Dawg and I enjoyed driving through the community. He was a fountain of community knowledge, and I learned a lot. Besides that, he was a savvy guy who knew not only the problems of the community but could clearly articulate many of the reasons for the problems.

I had seen the beautiful sandy Lake Michigan beaches of St. Joseph. "Let me take you to the beach set aside for the black people," he said. He directed me down a bad road lined with weeds to a shabby park in disarray, with unfinished buildings. "They gave us some money, but it ran out before the buildings could be finished."

"Do you see that baseball diamond?" He pointed to a beautifully groomed field near a local industry. "That's a private ball park for the employees and their families. It's nicer than any ball diamond in Benton Harbor. The little black kids can go play ball in the sand lots."

A short time later, Dawg commented, "There's a drug deal going down." And he was right. A police car came into view, seemingly from nowhere, and officers made an arrest.

"That house is a crack house," he said as he nodded toward a structure that was once a fine home. People walking in and out of the house sullenly watched the Toyota sedan pass by with a white man at the wheel and a black man in the passenger seat.

"See that woman? Look what drugs did to her!" As we approached from behind, the body appeared to be that of a very young girl. I turned around as we passed and was shocked to see that her face was that of an old, old woman.

"I went to school with that cop," he said, pointing to a nearby police cruiser. "That kid was dealing drugs when he was in school, and he's still dealing drugs. This police department has got some problems!"

> *Nobody knows the trouble I've seen,*
> *Nobody knows but Jesus.*[16]

Because of his problems with the law, Dawg would never get appointed to a position of influence in his community. Dawg was well dressed, well spoken, nice looking, and likeable; but most of all he had a real grasp of the community's needs and problems. What a waste of a wonderful resource.

Instead, the existing power structure made certain that only the "right" people were chosen to serve as liaison with the Governor's office. This would only ensure that the problems would not go away.

Dawg also worked closely with the students of David Protess, but they weren't able to push him beyond a certain point, either. He refused to go with their team to Ohio, to confront his Uncle Billy Lee (although he went there alone and attempted to get him to talk about it in a roundabout way). He would not let the team interview his mother or his relatives.

On June 6, 2003 the Medill Innocence Project team went to Ohio on their own, and they even managed to find and speak with Billy Lee for a few minutes. Brown seemed to remember nothing, but we found it significant that he also denied nothing.

Protess finally gave up and assigned his students to other projects.

Dawg and I drifted apart. He knew what was right, and what he should do, but crossing that line would very likely result in a permanent split with his own family and his peers. And that's all he had.

Would we ever get a break in this case?

In mid-2003, Maurice Carter's legal team, considered one of the finest in the country, filed a brief in support of its motion for the state to grant a new trial. A noted legal expert who read the brief said openly that it was one of the finest pieces of legal work he had seen. The Berrien County Prosecutor's Office didn't see it that way, however; they told the state and the media that the Carter brief was "artfully crafted and deceptively thorough," but didn't establish "a significant possibility of his innocence." The conclusion: Maurice did not deserve a new trial.

Assistant Prosecutor Wild was even bold enough to include in her brief that Maurice had confessed to another inmate that he had committed the crime. Little did she know that we had a surprise for her that would disprove that claim.

It was time for the Citizens Committee for the Release of Maurice Carter to stage another media event.

Rubin "Hurricane" Carter agreed to return to Benton Harbor. ("I'll keep coming back to Benton Harbor time after time until we get that man out of jail!" he declared.) We scheduled a press conference for Thursday, June 19, 2003, at which time Rubin would disclose to the media that we were holding an affidavit from inmate Jonathan Plain admitting that his signed statement held by the Prosecutor claiming that Carter had confessed the crime was a lie, and, further, that he had never met Maurice Carter.

In planning the event, we received an extra bonus. The Illegals Motorcycle Club, part of the Criminal Lawyers' Association of Toronto, would also come roaring into Benton Harbor on that day to support Rubin and to participate in the press conference. This most unusual motorcycle gang included in its membership two of Toronto's finest criminal defense attorneys, Paul Copeland and Phil Campbell. Both are board members for the Association in Defence of the Wrongly Convicted, which had endorsed the Carter case. We were sure the media would love this.

Each spring the bikers, garbed in leather, and riding colorful motorcycles of various model and brand, roar out of Toronto on what they call a "freedom ride." In June, 2002,

Rubin "Hurricane" Carter with Paul Copeland, prominent Toronto criminal defense attorney

the Illegals traveled to Harrisburg, Pennsylvania, where they helped free Steven Crawford, who had spent twenty-eight years in prison for a murder he did not commit. This year they would try to do the same for Maurice Carter, asking for a private visit with Prosecutor Cherry and announcing that they would participate in the Rubin Carter press conference. The prosecutor would never agree to meet with a gang like this, but they were headed to Michigan anyway.

We were enthusiastic and made extensive plans for the day. We reserved rooms on Wednesday evening at the Clarion Inn in St. Joseph, where a press conference could be held on Thursday.

Learning that Rubin would be arriving at midday on Wednesday, June 18, we made arrangements with the local movie house in Benton Harbor to show the film *The Hurricane* that night. With the genuine Hurricane actually in the audience, ready to answer questions and sign autographs, we believed we had a crowd pleaser in the making.

Talk about attracting the media.

Little did we realize at the time how far and wide our story would travel.

> *Deep and wide,*
> *Deep and wide,*
> *There's a fountain flowing*
> *deep and wide.*[17]

The Pot Boils Over

Take a large pot and throw in such ingredients as years and years of wrongful convictions, excessive criminal charges against persons of color, excessive sentences for persons of color, racial profiling by local police agencies, other forms of police harassment, rampant poverty, high unemployment, serious drug problems, and a general atmosphere of racism.

Let it simmer for years unchecked, and I'll guarantee that no matter how low the flame, someday that pot's going to boil over. Benton Harbor was about to.

Sunday nights are generally uneventful for police officers on patrol, but at 2:00 a.m., Monday, June 16, a call on his police radio caught the attention of Benton Township officer Wesley Koza. A Berrien County Sheriff's deputy was involved in a high-speed chase that began on U.S. 31 near Scottdale, Michigan. A short time later, realizing he couldn't catch the fleeing motorcycle, the deputy abandoned the chase near I-94. Officer Koza suspected the bike might be heading his way, and shortly he spotted the motorcycle. He activated his emergency lights and siren and gave chase.

Generally speaking, police patrol cars are a poor match for a speedy motorcycle. That was certainly true for the Benton Township cop car. The motorcycle sped across the city limits. Blocks behind came the chugging township cruiser. Motorcyclist Terrance Shurn unwisely guided his rocket into the inner city. Here no amount of driving skill would help the biker. Shurn's speed was too much for the streets in the 'hood. He lost control of his motorcycle; it jumped a curb and sailed into an abandoned house. Silence. Then the sound of a siren as the police car approached. Terrance Devon "T-shirt" Shurn was dead at the age of 27.

The story spread quickly through the inner city, where people gather on street corners, in party store parking lots, on rickety front porches, and under dim street lights, drinking and smoking products of their choice, and talking about "things." Often grumbling. Because of the action of a white cop, a black man was dead.

Officer Wesley Koza could not have imagined that this very accident would create the breeze that fanned the flame that caused the pot to boil over.

Residents of the neighborhood related later that mob mentality took over, cars were overturned, houses were torched. Anger that had been suppressed for decades finally exploded. No more! They were going to take it no more.

I've worked in the newsroom and I know the feeling when local news converts into national news, almost instantly. Giant television network satellite trucks and reporters from all over the country descended on this little town, hellbent to get sensational pictures, copy, and interviews. Their early morning stories and pictures would boost ratings and readership and would heap more shame and scorn on the already scarred Benton Harbor.

Said *Detroit Free Press* writer David Zeman, "History has sadly repeated itself in the fractious and impoverished community of Benton Harbor." [18] He was referring to widespread rioting that occurred in the same community in August, 1966. The fatal shooting of a black teenager by a gunman in a passing car was blamed for starting that outbreak. The reasons given for those riots sounded very familiar: aggressive police tactics, a lack of jobs, and a lack of recreational opportunities for young blacks. Remember the words of Dawg?

The *Washington Post* quoted statistics saying that a third of the households in this city of 12,000 people had incomes of less than $10,000, and 50 percent of those sixteen and older were unemployed.

Those who have read the book written by Alex Kotlowitz will remember the skepticism about police conduct in this community, as officers investigated the death of black teenager Eric McGinnis. Kotlowitz was soon contacted at his home near Chicago about these riots, and his first thoughts were that all of this was happening because of Maurice.

That reaction was more accurate than one might think. Some reporters told me later that they were amazed how often the name of Maurice Carter had come up when they interviewed the general public about reasons for the rioting. Many said that it all started back in the 1970s "when that cop was shot." [19]

Scott Elliott, chairman of our citizens committee, was quoted in the *Toronto Star* as saying that Maurice Carter's case lies "at the very heart and soul" of decades of civic decline and racial strife in his community.

> *Ain't gonna study war no more,*
> *Ain't gonna study war no more,*
> *Ain't gonna study war no more!* [20]

The rioting continued a second night, but by then most of the stories and pictures had been told and shown. Reporters began their quest for new copy material. Our timing for a Maurice Carter news event could not have been more perfect.

Completely unaware of the seriousness of the problem down south, I stopped for a doughnut on my way to Grand Rapids Wednesday morning, the day Rubin Carter and the Illegals were scheduled to arrive in Michigan. I blinked! On the convenience store television screen, *CNN News* showed the words "Benton Harbor, Michigan" over footage of burning houses and cars. Color photographs of riot scenes with giant headlines on the front of the *Detroit News* and the *Detroit Free Press* jumped out at me from the outdoor newspaper vending machines. My heart nearly leaped into my throat!

This is just what we don't need, Lord! If the city is torn up by riots, how is our little case going to get any media attention?

Should we still go ahead? I hurried to make telephone calls to committee members in Berrien County.

Actually, there was little we could do. Rubin was already on an airplane out of Toronto. And the Illegals had left Toronto the previous Friday, taking a circuitous route to southwestern Michigan through several southern states. Knowing this gang—Rubin and the Illegals—they wouldn't miss the action in Benton Harbor for all the money in the world anyway.

Rubin Carter doesn't have a particular love for police officers. He arrived wide-eyed at the Clarion Hotel in St. Joseph, where the parking lot overflowed with Michigan State Police cars, and the hotel lobby was swarming with uniformed officers. The Michigan State Police and the Michigan National Guard had been ordered into the city to restore order. Their temporary headquarters and place of residence was the Clarion Hotel.

Later the Illegals arrived. The *Toronto Star* quoted the cyclists as saying that they rode into a town that was in a state of emergency, with "burned-down buildings, smashed windows, and an overwhelming military and police presence." [21]

Innocence Project codirectors Keith Findley and John Pray were driving to Benton Harbor from Madison, Wisconsin, with their law students. My cell phone rang as our growing crowd tried to get service in the Clarion restaurant. Keith Findley asked anxiously, "Is it safe to come?"

By the dinner hour we had a huge group in the dining room, and the hotel staff just wasn't prepared for this onslaught: state cops, national guardsmen, Maurice Carter supporters, and media representatives. I don't believe the Clarion had been this busy in months. As a result, dinner was slow in coming, which did nothing for my already sour mood. I was bummed. We had done such a great job of planning this media event, only to be topped by nationally publicized riots.

No fair, Lord. We were first!

Phil Campbell, one of the seven motorcycle riders (six men and one woman) asked if I had a copy of the documents filed in court on behalf of Maurice Carter. I checked with Keith Findley. He had a complete set, and we handed them over to Campbell. I learned that Phil is one of a rare breed of attorneys who limit their practice to wrongful conviction cases. First impression: big, burly motorcycle gang member. Lasting impression: eloquent writer and orator, and a genuine freedom fighter.

Plans still called for a showing of the movie *The Hurricane* at the only theater in Benton Harbor, safely located outside of the area of the riots. Rubin "Hurricane" Carter was scheduled to make a personal appearance. Scott Elliott went on ahead to make the necessary preparations. I tried to keep some semblance of order at the hotel.

Our waitress had bad news. There was a bomb threat at the theater, and the Michigan National Guard had opened the highway bridge between Benton Harbor and St. Joseph, effectively halting all traffic between the two communities. I made the decision that we could not jeopardize the lives of Rubin and our other guests. Besides, we were on the wrong side of the bridge. There was no way to get there. We would have to cancel.

An angry Scott Elliott was shouting at me over his cell phone. He was standing in the theater lobby with Benton Harbor Mayor Charles "Mickey" Yarborough. I had relayed the information we received from the waitress, and both Scott and the mayor were incensed. "One more example of St. Joseph starting rumors about Benton Harbor," they claimed.

The mayor flatly denied that there had been a bomb threat. Scott got on my case because people were gathering at the theater, representatives of the media were there, we were supposed to be there, and, the bridge was *not* open! They had both just crossed it into Benton Harbor. Even though some of our gang hadn't even been served yet, I shooed everyone out of the restaurant.

The show went on.

The crowd wasn't large, but our team was there, Rubin was there, the Illegals were there, and, most importantly, media representatives by now were hungry for alternate stories. Reporters and photographers were on the prowl, and we got some great press coverage.

OK, so I was wrong one more time. Thanks for the super coverage this evening.

I headed for home, and a hug, and a drink ... mentally and physically exhausted.

It was a short night. Early Thursday morning I returned to Benton Harbor in the rain. Very few Maurice Carter events drew the favor of the weatherman. Barrister Campbell met me at the hotel breakfast table. He had stayed up most of the night to read the entire University of Wisconsin legal team's brief on behalf of Maurice Carter. He couldn't praise the legal team enough. Later, in the noon press conference he told the media, "I have done a lot of this work, and have seen a lot of this work, a great deal of it well intentioned but ineffectively and ultimately futile. However, the brief filed before Judge Hammond on behalf of Maurice Carter is a splendid piece of advocacy. And that means, as we hit the Interstate tonight and head north to another part of Michigan, I do so personally with a great deal of confidence and hope that Maurice Carter will be freed."

He forgot one thing. We were in Berrien County.

Rain couldn't stop the motorcycle procession. They propped signs on their bikes or draped "Free Maurice Carter" T-shirts over their saddle bags. Members of the citizens committee followed in their cars with signs in all the windows. We were headed to the regular meeting of the Berrien County Board of Commissioners, but we made a detour so that the motorcade could travel through the chic downtown district of St. Joseph—four-way lights flashing, horns blaring—then on to the county building where the commissioners were meeting. While some commissioners and officials were trying to get Rubin Carter autographs and pictures, others were nervously debating whether they should let us in. The room was small and certain restrictions were in effect. Permission was soon granted, but conditions were imposed that limited the number of speakers and the length of the speeches.

Most memorable were the words from the Hurricane and the Canadian attorneys. Phil Campbell was particularly miffed that he and his cohorts had ridden all that distance only to be rebuffed by the Prosecutor. He told the commissioners: "We do not want to turn the exoneration of Maurice Carter into a public relations or a political exercise … we prefer to sit down with the prosecutors and speak to them lawyer-to-lawyer and tell them our concerns about this. They have refused."

No comment from that august body.

Back to the hotel for the news conference. The media people were looking for new angles, and the riot stories were getting old. Our conference was an unqualified success. This looked like the big time! The room was filled with television cameras and lights, radio broadcasters with microphones, and newspaper reporters accompanied by their photographers. Of course every reporter wanted something exclusive, so many of us were getting pulled into a corner or a corridor for a private interview. Our son, Matthew, a fledgling sports reporter for our local newspaper, had one of the finest experiences of his early career. I had arranged for Matt to interview Rubin in his hotel room. The Hurricane was most gracious, and a thrilled Matthew went back to his newspaper with an exclusive. Hey, I was a young reporter once, and I'm a dad now. Would I pull strings for my son? In the twinkling of an eye!

Members of the Wisconsin Innocence Project team wore their
"Free Maurice Carter" shirts to good advantage.

Once again the clergy stood together as a group showing
solidarity on the Carter issue. It was a strong statement to
the media. Anyone who had ever attended a meeting of the
Citizens Committee for the Release of Maurice Carter was
proud to show up today.

Then came the Hurricane.

First, he read the entire affidavit from Jonathan Plain, the
inmate who recanted his testimony, and media representatives heard for the first time about the maneuverings that had
taken place to elicit a false accusation.

In the question-and-answer session, Hurricane was asked
about the riots.

"This reminds me of what was going on thirty-seven years
ago when I was convicted for a crime that I didn't commit,"
said Rubin to a reporter for the *Toledo Blade*. "This is what
happens when you allow the affluent to live on one side of
the river and leave the other side in poverty." [22]

The Governor Drops By

Word suddenly spread through the media representatives present that Michigan Governor Jennifer Granholm was headed to Benton Harbor that afternoon. She promised a press briefing late in the day but first agreed to hold a public hearing with the citizens of Benton Harbor, sans media, at the Brotherhood of All Nations Church of God in Christ. That was the church of the Rev. James Atterberry, who had shown support of our cause in the past. Prominent Democrats in our circles and friends of Atterberry felt that we could get into the meeting, especially if Rubin Carter wished to attend. I was Rubin's driver, so I asked him. I knew that he was tiring. "Give me an hour in my hotel room," he said. "Then pick me up."

Scott Elliott did a superb job, and we gained admission without a problem. Parking was at a premium as the television satellite behemoths jammed the dirt roads around the inner-city church. The governor had promised to hold the press conference right outside the building following the private hearing. With Scott making the introductions, Rubin and I passed all barricades. An aide to the governor quickly arranged for the two of us to have just a few seconds of Granholm's time before the hearing began. Rubin presented the governor with a copy of the affidavit. Naturally that wasn't the primary thing on her mind right then, but she handed it to an aide and instructed him to take care of it. She gave me a firm handshake, listened to me for a minute with eyes locked on mine, and promised to consider our issue later. I was impressed with her response, but I had worked with too many politicians to get my hopes up.

The people in the crowded church poured out their hearts to the governor, and she seemed as if she heard their cries and sympathized with them. That's what she told the media in her press conference; but history shows that, for the most part, it was politics as usual when everything settled down.

Blessed are the poor in spirit,
for theirs is the kingdom of heaven.

—Matthew 5:13

Rubin and I stood behind the governor during the outdoor conference. Television cameras that aimed at her caught our faces as well.

The two of us were scheduled to do a radio broadcast that evening before I headed home, and Rubin refused. He was too tired. It made no difference that we had committed to doing this. He insisted that I take him back to the hotel. I was just the driver; he made the decisions.

The interviewer was furious. His tirade nearly melted my cell phone. He tried to change Rubin's mind and, when that didn't work, he unleashed his frustration on me. Not only was I helpless, but I was also exhausted. I was heading home with a smile on my face. Mission accomplished!

The next time we spoke, Maurice was anxious to hear my retelling of the events of June 19. If I didn't know better, I could have sworn that Maurice had a little nip of the fruit of the vine. I know that he doesn't drink, although he has always claimed that *anything* is available in prison for a price. His speech seemed a bit slower, and I thought that he was slurring a little bit on some of his words. It must have been my imagination, I reasoned.

I reminded him that I would be heading north to vacation for two weeks, so we could not have our twice-a-week telephone conversations. He encouraged us to have a good time, relax, and not to worry.

Things didn't turn out that way.

Camping was not easy, but it was necessary. Most of our family traveled north to Leelanau Pines, a campground on Lake

Leelanau just outside of the little town of Cedar in northern Michigan, a heavenly spot where we would try to unwind for two weeks.

The first week I was rather ill, but I could think of no better place to recover.

Because our case was in the hands of Judge Hammond, I maintained e-mail contact with all of our people once a day. I had found some friends in the park who had a telephone line. With their permission, I brought the laptop computer to their camper every day to collect and send messages.

Having gone downstate for a weekend wedding, Marcia and I were back in the campground on Sunday. I later recorded in my daily countdown that we were being ushered into perhaps one of the darkest weeks in our history with Maurice Carter.

It all began with a telephone call.

Lisa Connell was on the line, obviously crying, her words unintelligible due to a poor connection. Cellular telephone service in the park is poor at best. I ran to the shore of Lake Leelanau, where the signal picks up additional strength from a high tower near Traverse City.

Maurice had suffered a stroke.

No, Lord, no! Not now! Not when we've come this far! The end is in sight!

Terry Kelly had received a call from within the prison. The only thing she could find out was that his illness was not life-threatening. Despite a flurry of telephone calls, we could find out no more.

I got an early start Monday morning and drew on all of my contacts by telephone: our Michigan Attorney Gary Giguere, Lisa, Scott, the prison chaplain, the prison's assistant administrator, the public information office of the Michigan Department of Corrections, and *Grand Rapids Press* staff writer Pat Shellenbarger.

We learned that Maurice had been moved from the Thumb Correctional Facility, but information as to his new location was scarce.

When I arrived home on Saturday evening, Maurice called me and I managed to extract the information from him as to what happened. He sounded so tired, so weak, and yet he wanted to talk first about my family and about his case. All I wanted to do was find out what the heck was going on with his health.

Finally, the story.

The problems had started a week earlier, the prior Saturday, when he tried to take a walk, a part of his daily exercise. He had to stop and sit down, and he actually passed out for a minute. One of the prison workers happened by. "You all right, Mr. Carter?" He wasn't.

Sunday he collapsed again (not a stroke), was treated at the prison clinic, and was returned to the general population. It was determined that he should be taken to the Lapeer Regional Hospital.

Maurice said that his 4-day stay there was like a visit to hell. Despite the seriousness of his condition, he was shackled to the bed and a guard was placed in his room, according to policy. They gave him water pills, or diuretics, as a part of the treatment. This makes the patient urinate with some frequency, not very convenient when you're tied to the bed. If the guard happened to be a friendly guard, he worked with Maurice to promptly get him to the restroom. If the guard chose to be ornery that day, Maurice could just wait until this individual felt like getting up and unlocking the chains.

Maurice informed me that he still didn't have his medical report, but he had heard enough from the doctors and nurses to know that he had low blood pressure and was anemic. That information set alarms ringing in the mind of the hospice nurse/parish nurse with whom I share a bed.

Maurice was back in the general population by the time he called me on that Saturday evening, July 26. I was determined to go see him, but he discouraged me from driving to Lapeer the next day. He needed rest. I reluctantly agreed, knowing that it was a long walk from his cell to the visiting area. He didn't sound up to it.

Our parting messages of "I love you" seemed more meaningful this time.

Much of our discussion at the citizens committee meeting the following Monday centered on the health of Maurice Carter, but even the immediate family had no additional information.

The story gets worse.

It was Wednesday morning, July 30; I had already left for my office in Grand Rapids. The telephone rang at home and Marcia took her time answering because that's about the time the telemarketers start their barrage of sales calls. This morning, however, it was a collect call from the Thumb Correctional Facility from Maurice Carter. Marcia accepted the call, but the voice on the other end was *not* that of Maurice Carter.

The man identified himself as Jerry, Maurice's "bunkie," the prison term for roommate. Maurice was in bad shape, disoriented, acting strangely. Maurice wanted me to know what was going on, but couldn't remember my telephone number (evidence enough that things weren't good!). Together they found our number and Maurice's PIN to make the collect call. Jerry described the symptoms to Marcia, who responded that he must go to the infirmary right away. Jerry petulantly stated that if I had visited Maurice on Sunday I would have noticed that he needed help.

Then Maurice spoke briefly with Marcia. She repeated the orders to him: Infirmary, now!

I salute Jerry Talison, Inmate #119-546, date of birth 11/26/47. Sentence: life. Charge: first degree murder. I know nothing about the man taking a life. I know for certain that he saved one.

Marcia called me, and that triggered the next flurry of telephone calls. We learned that the infirmary personnel were going to send Maurice back to his cell again, and we rebelled. Pastor Gulley got through to someone at the governor's office—a contact that he had made in the aftermath of the riots. Gulley's message to the governor: "If you think you had a problem in Benton Harbor over a motorcycle accident, wait 'til you see what happens if you let this poor black man die in prison!"

Orders came down from the top in no time. Maurice Carter would be transferred to the Duane L. Waters Hospital, in the Egeler complex, a part of the Michigan prison system.

The next day I received a call on my cell phone from the medical social worker assigned to Maurice Carter, who informed me that Maurice Carter had been diagnosed with liver disease, *end stage!* It was hepatitis C.

How long did he have to live?

A matter-of-fact response: "Perhaps a few weeks, maybe months."

They would try to get him well enough to return him to the general population.

Medical records that we obtained much later revealed that prison doctors had diagnosed the hepatitis C as early as 1995 but had done nothing about it. Apparently, if the patient doesn't know he's sick, he doesn't require any treatment.

With tears in my eyes I immediately dialed the number of Keith Findley. We had to try to persuade the courts to hurry up. If Maurice Carter was going to die, we wanted him to die a free man. Keith promised to contact Gary Giguere, and together they would get the ball rolling.

Could I visit Maurice?

No, every time a prisoner gets transferred to a new facility, there is a 30-day period before he can have visitors. I'm a member of the clergy. You mean a guy can't see his own pastor when he's dying? Rules are rules.

We'll see about that.

Meanwhile I learned that the transfer occurred so quickly that some of Maurice Carter's belongings were left behind. This meant that I had to make one more trip to the Thumb Correctional Facility. My last drive to Lapeer was not a pleasant one. His personal possessions had been stuffed into two large plastic bags by a kind, unknown, but caring woman down in housekeeping. I thanked her, struggled back to the car, plopped the heavy bags into the trunk, and steered back onto the highway.

Baiting the "Trap"

Reporters learn to become innovative. There was no way I would abide by the prison's rule and wait thirty days to see Maurice in the prison hospital. I discovered that the assistant administrator's last name was Trapp. My mother's maiden name was Trap, and some of her relatives spelled their name with two ps instead of one. So the first thing I did was start up a conversation about his name and my mom's maiden name. We were soon chatting like old friends.

Then I explained that I had clergy status and wanted to visit Mr. Carter. He looked it up, saw no problem with that, and asked when I would like to come. I gave him a day, date and time, and he said he would inform the front desk. He held up his end of the bargain, and I breezed through the visitor procedures at the Duane L. Waters Hospital.

The building looks quite nice until you get past the front doors. I couldn't have known how many more times I would be traveling to this hospital within the next year, and I learned to hate the place. The people were always nice to me, but the facilities were terrible, the treatment was almost nonexistent, and the visiting area was despicable. Certainly, our state could do better.

When you visit any of the regular prison facilities in Michigan, unless the prisoners are in maximum security, you sit together in a large room filled with chairs. The atmosphere is pleasant, the chairs are comfortable, the temperature is reasonable, and a guard sitting on a platform at one end of the room is, if not genial, at least accommodating.

But, when you visit an inmate at the prison hospital, you are ushered into a barren little room with glass on all sides. The floor is not carpeted. There are steel benches in the room with no back rests. The prisoner must sit on one bench to face his visitor, who sits across from him on another of these cushionless benches. Guards and other hospital personnel keep an eye on things through the many windows, a miserable way to visit.

My heart sank as I saw Maurice come shuffling into the room. He didn't look good. I didn't stay long. The seating was too uncomfortable for this ailing inmate. We hugged, did our "I love you" goodbyes, and I was in the car making the nearly 3-hour drive back home.

The hospital telephone system wasn't so hot, either. It was some time before we could establish a routine. Prison staffers were of little assistance, so for a while we just could not communicate.

That wasn't the only punishment to be suffered by this patient man.

His radio, his little black-and-white television set, his typewriter, his beard trimmer (he was always particular about his appearance) and even his partial dental plate didn't catch up with him in the hospital for quite some time. So there he was, locked in his little room with nothing to do each day. He couldn't call me, he couldn't listen to the radio, he couldn't watch TV, he couldn't even type a letter on those days when his motor skills began to improve. Worse than that, he was ashamed of his appearance. His beard wasn't trimmed, and he despised being seen by family or friends with some of his teeth missing.

Our questions were legion. What kind of treatment for hepatitis C would he receive in the prison system? The quick answer: stopgap only. The drug that Maurice needed is called Interferon, and the medical social worker was quick to inform us that it's too expensive. The State of Michigan would not treat him with it. Is there any way that Maurice Carter can survive? His only hope is a liver transplant. May he be evaluated for a transplant? No. There are only two hospitals in Michigan where transplants are performed, the University of Michigan and Henry Ford Hospital, one public and one private. Neither, however, will evaluate prisoners for transplants. All the more reason to speed up the process to free Maurice Carter.

Maurice did respond to the treatment that he was receiving, and social worker Scott Morgan informed me that our patient would soon be transferred to a different unit. Maurice asked for a transfer to another unit right there in the Egeler complex, called C Unit. That way he would be near the hospital and the medical staff. But that was too simple. In their infinite wisdom, the Michigan Department of Corrections planners chose to send him to a medical floor at the Lakeland Facility in Coldwater, the prison where I first met Maurice. It's a long drive.

The transfer to Coldwater had one bright spot. Because he had been in Lakeland before, some of his old friends were still there. I developed admiration for some of the things that happen in the prison community. Maurice's old friends took care of him. One in particular, a Christian by the name of Wayne Gilmore, kind of took him under his wings. He went way above and beyond the call of duty to take good care of my brother, and Maurice was very grateful to him.

Alas, Maurice Carter was not able to remain in Coldwater for long. His caregivers, if you can call them that, didn't monitor his diet closely, and didn't enforce a strict routine of taking his medication. And, so, it was only a matter of time before Maurice's condition worsened. He was rushed back to Duane L. Waters Hospital.

I have a friend whose father was a prison warden. He said he was happy that he never had to be admitted to the Duane L. Waters Hospital.

I have another friend who is an inmate in a facility in the Upper Peninsula. He says prisoners throughout the Michigan system are terrorized by the thought of having to go to Duane L. Waters Hospital. The rumor among the prison population is that you don't receive treatment there, you get sent there to die. This prisoner said that if you should have the bad luck of getting sent to Waters with a medical problem, and the good luck to get released again someday, you'd go back to your cell with a different medical problem. Inmates will lie and claim their illness is gone before allowing the MDOC to send them to Waters.

And the Duane L. Waters Hospital was once again the home for Maurice Carter.

The Carter legal team hustled to put together a new request to the Court. In September, they filed documents asking that a hearing on whether Maurice Carter should have a new trial be sped up. Medical information was included describing his fragile condition. No immediate response.

Maurice's cousin Mary Blackwell played a key role in keeping Maurice as healthy as possible. She and I could both detect through phone conversations the subtle signs of elevated ammonia level, something that happens when a person's liver isn't doing its job. Maurice's speech would become slurred and he would become forgetful. That meant that he needed attention quickly. Failure to do anything about this would result in an even higher ammonia level, which ultimately could result in another coma. There were times when Mary had to call someone as high up as the Medical Director of the Michigan Department of Corrections. And she would do it in the blink of an eye if she felt that things weren't happening to her satisfaction at a lower level. Mary was and is a fighter, and her involvement at this time in Maurice's life was invaluable.

It was one of those times when Maurice didn't sound good, and I was worried. I drove to Jackson. I was promptly processed at the front desk, but then there was a problem. A meeting was being held in the visitation room. The guard that was escorting me quickly conferred with some other official people. He informed me that I would have to visit Mr. Carter in his hospital room. (Maurice later informed me that I was probably the first civilian ever to be permitted on the hospital floor. Perhaps that's why, after just a few minutes, officials at a higher level ordered both of us to return to the visitor quarters. The meeting was over.)

That's when I discovered that the Duane L. Waters Hospital looks good only on the outside. Maintenance has been poor on the inside. The elevator that we took to the second floor was actually missing pieces of flooring. The second floor housed the Intensive Care Unit, and I was horrified to notice that my escort had to unlock the hospital room door. When he opened the door, I was horrified again. This wasn't the Maurice Carter that I was accustomed to seeing. There was only one chair, so he sat on the edge of the bed. It was chilly in the room.

I drove from Jackson to Benton Harbor for a meeting of the citizens committee. My candid report shocked everyone. My guts were still burning, churning, the next morning. I wanted Carter supporters to be angry, also. I sent the following message via e-mail to more than 200 people who believed in our cause:

> Maurice Carter is 59. I visited an old man yesterday. I was shocked when I walked into his tiny hospital room in Jackson. This was not the same Maurice Carter, the one with a quick smile, and quick step, and impeccable dress.
>
> An 80-year-old man appeared to be sitting on the bed with hands shaking. It was too much effort to get up to welcome me. His voice was weak, and his memory came and went.
>
> The stark hospital room contained a small bed, a small chair, and a toilet. No TV. No radio. He owns both appliances, but the prison system isn't very quick to transfer belongings.
>
> And, besides freedom, do you know what he wants? A blanket! It's cold on that hospital floor, in contrast to the hospitals that you and I enjoy. He gets a standard issue of hospital gown, robe, socks, and a blanket on the bed. He can't get warm. His medical social worker is "looking into" the possibility of getting him another blanket.
>
> For the first time, he expresses some doubt that all of this is going to work out. I tried to give him faith, saying that we expect something to happen this week, either from the judge or the governor.
>
> When I departed, the guards saw two grown men hugging and weeping, expressing their love for each other.

> This would be cruel and unusual punishment even for someone guilty of a crime. For an innocent man who has been in prison for nearly 28 years, it is unconscionable!

Well, at least I got it out of my system. Reaction was swift. My little report appeared in a couple of newspapers. *Chicago Tribune* columnist Eric Zorn put the whole thing on his website.

On October 29, 2003, Maurice Carter's supporters and legal team were in a Berrien County Circuit Court room. Keep in mind that this was not the *big* date. A hearing first had to be conducted on our request to expedite the hearing on our motion for a new trial. We were about to get a taste of more Berrien County justice.

Judge Hammond arrived in the courtroom, and we were granted permission to be seated. He started rambling on about the Maurice Carter case, and it soon became apparent that he didn't realize why we were there. He used the excuse that he's very busy, and people tell him what case he must hear, the time and the date. He actually thought he was in the courtroom to consider our request for a new trial. Confusion was written across his face when Assistant Prosecutor Beth Wild explained that this was merely the hearing on the request to expedite.

Our head counsel, Keith Findley, tried to stress the urgency of hurrying the Maurice Carter case along. "Our concern is … he could take a turn and die tomorrow," he said.

Judge Hammond's response: "Most of us could die tomorrow."

Snapped Keith: "Not of liver disease!"

In an interview with Pat Shellenbarger of *The Grand Rapids Press* after the court session, Judge Hammond commented, "Everybody dies sooner or later, anyway."

The judge kept insisting that we could start the hearing on our motion for a new trial right then. Our legal team was quite delighted with that, saying they were prepared to proceed. That's when Beth Wild went into a tizzy. She wasn't ready for that hearing. She had been holding us at arm's length for nearly a year. She needed more time.

"How soon can you be ready—in an hour?" the judge asked.

With panic in her voice, Wild asked for a recess to confer with her boss.

Gary Giguere and Keith Findley caught me in the hallway outside the courtroom. "What would you think of asking Cherry for a deal? Both sides go to the court and suggest that Maurice be given credit for time served. He could be free right away."

I responded favorably, but reminded them that they must first check with Mary to see how the family felt about this.

This had been a sensitive subject in the past because Maurice had stubbornly refused to consider that kind of a deal. He correctly argued that after being freed he would still be a convicted felon, and he didn't want to be serving as the executive director of INNOCENT! with that on his record. He wanted and deserved a clean slate.

Maurice had told me, "I can just see us driving somewhere in the State of Texas and getting stopped by the cops. When they see on the computer that I was convicted of shooting a police officer we might not make it out of the state without bullet holes in our car!"

The situation, of course, was different this time. Now it was a matter of life and death. He needed a liver transplant, and if he didn't get it, he would die.

Mary concurred, and attorney Gary Giguere ran upstairs to the Prosecutor's office. I prayed, but didn't get the answer I wanted.

Is anything going to go right today, Lord?

Gary was back within minutes, and the look on his face told the whole story. He had been shooed out of James Cherry's office. We had started this whole thing, now we would live with it right to the bitter end. No deal.

We returned to the courtroom.

The Prosecutor's office was not prepared to go ahead with the hearing. Besides, Wild had promised members of the Schadler family that they could attend the hearing, and the Schadlers were not present today.

Hearing that the Schadlers would be attending the hearing, our attorneys responded by saying they wanted Maurice Carter brought to the courtroom, as well. That prompted the judge to make another of his outlandish comments. Saying that if Maurice Carter was as ill as we were claiming, he might not survive the ride to Benton Harbor. Joked the judge: "I don't own a term policy on his life … it doesn't do me any good to endanger his life."

Assistant Prosecutor Wild got in another lick by saying that, for the record, her office opposed speeding up the process, despite the fact that Maurice was failing.

Judge Hammond disregarded that and set the hearing for November 12.

My notes in the daily countdown diary that day read: "I left Benton Harbor in a state of shock, feeling like I needed a shower."

Grand Rapids Press writer Pat Shellenbarger was appalled, saying it was the most bizarre courtroom experience he ever had in his career as a reporter. [23]

Said *Chicago Tribune* columnist Eric Zorn: "I've seen and heard a lot of callous indifference from officials in my years of covering criminal justice issues, but Wednesday's flip remark by Berrien County Circuit Judge John Hammond may well be the most infamous." [24]

Editorialized Ed Golder in *The Grand Rapids Press*: "Re-
opening a case should be reserved for extraordinary circumstances. Maurice Carter is that rare instance. A jury should
hear his case again, with all the evidence this time. Refusing
him that right is an insult—almost as much as the cheap jokes
and ill-considered comments from the bench." [25]

> *Where are the clowns? Quick, send in the clowns.*
> *Don't bother, they're here.* [26]

I relayed the information to Maurice the next time he
called, the crude remarks by the insensitive judge, the rude
rejection of a deal offer by the prosecutor.

"I told you so!"

Judge Hammond seemed to watch his words much more
carefully when we appeared in court on November 12, 2003.
Television cameras were present.

I hated the feeling in that courtroom. I hated the sight of
the judge. I hated the attitude of the assistant prosecutor. I
hated the smug looks on the faces of the Schadler family. I
hated the fact that we hadn't listened to Maurice on those
two key issues: the venue and the judge.

As I mentioned earlier, however, we had the media. And we
had spectators. The tiny courtroom was filled to capacity.

Judge Hammond briefly reviewed the case, acknowledged
that Maurice was now ill, and then reviewed Maurice's earlier
appeals, all of which had been denied.

Then he gave each side thirty minutes to present opposing
arguments.

Keith Findley was well prepared and did a terrific job. The
fact that the judge wasn't paying any attention to him didn't
seem to bother him at all.

Beth Wild's presentation was exactly the opposite. There were awkward pauses, and it appeared that she hadn't spent much time on preparation.

Our 2-inch-thick stack of documents reflected the unbelievable amount of work in preparation for this session. Even though we suspected that the judge never looked at the material, we hoped that he would not rule today. Instead, we wanted an evidentiary hearing. Keith explained that such a hearing would be very much like a trial because we would put every witness on the stand. It could very well run for a week. We would view that hearing as a victory.

Judge Hammond announced a 30-minute recess.

When he returned he began reading a typewritten statement. That document, which sounded amazingly similar to the prosecutor's summary, couldn't have been prepared in thirty minutes! His decision had been made and printed out before the arguments were even heard.

No evidentiary hearing.

Request for a new trial denied.

> *The world treat you mean, Lord;*
> *Treat me mean, too.*
> *But that's how things is down here ...* [27]

The look of defeat on Keith's face said it all. Some of the students started crying. The African-American spectators seemed to share one facial expression that said, "What else did you expect? We get this every time!"

On the other side of the aisle, members of the Schadler family were laughing, back-slapping, and shaking hands. I was mystified. These people are elated about keeping a deathly ill inmate behind bars?

All members of the legal group and all members of the citizens committee were surrounded by reporters. Gary Giguere

announced that the appellate process would begin immediately, but what were the lay people supposed to say? We had
nothing to talk about.

My only response to the questions of interviewers was that
the outcome was exactly as Maurice Carter had predicted.
He did not expect to find justice in Berrien County.

When I finally walked into the elevator, I could hold back
the tears no longer.

As I stood by the car buffeted by the strong, cold winds
off Lake Michigan, Lisa Connell came running up. She had
a birthday gift for me from the committee, a beautifully
wrapped bottle of single malt Scotch.

We looked at each other, a team of two who had worked so
hard to free Maurice, unable to speak. We hugged. We sobbed.
We broke apart and she silently dashed to her car.

Scott Elliott walked over and tried to cheer me up. "We're
not going to give up. We're going to fight harder than ever."

I slammed the car door and sat in silence. Finally I dialed
home on the cell phone: "We lost."

This ride to Spring Lake was a long one. Maurice was
scheduled to call at 7:00 p.m. for the outcome. One of the
few negative things to be said about this beautiful relationship between Maurice Carter and Doug Tjapkes was that it
was *always* my duty to be the messenger, and more often than
not, it seemed lately, the news wasn't good. I wasn't looking
forward to the call on the evening of November 12.

Having said all of that, I must stress one more time what
a gentleman this man was. And my comments to the media
were accurate. He was not surprised. Keith and the entire
team asked me to relay their apologies to him. He, in turn,
asked me to thank them for their hours and days and weeks
and years (four of them!) invested in this single project. Then
he prodded me on. We had work to do.

After Marcia and I hugged and cried, she went out to get us some Chinese food.

I typed in the sad news on the computer keyboard for the e-mail network.

I decided to sample the single-malt Scotch.

Reaction was immediate, and often acerbic, such as the headline of the *Chicago Tribune* column by Eric Zorn: "Justice goes up in smoke along with new trial." [28]

The attorneys scurried to prepare an appeal, which was filed in December with the Michigan Court of Appeals in Grand Rapids.

Worried by Maurice's increasingly frequent problems with liver disease along with the ominous predictions of how long he might survive, supporters launched an all-out effort to seek a commutation of his sentence by the governor. We were informed that the Michigan Parole Board first reviews a request for commutation and then makes a recommendation to the governor. While the governor is not bound to follow that recommendation, that's usually the way it goes because the parole board allegedly does the investigative homework.

More bad news. The Michigan Parole Board, unconvinced by numerous editorials in major newspapers, voted 7 to 2 against recommending a commutation of the sentence for medical reasons. No word from the governor's office.

The longer this goes on, the less I understand of your plan. Please don't let him die behind bars. Please.

Bon Appetit!

"Hey Big Bro, the next time you come to see me, bring in a bunch of quarters so we can get ourselves something to eat." I am ashamed to admit that I had been making prison visits for perhaps a decade and never gave it a thought that the inmate I visited might enjoy food from the vending machines.

The walls of the visitation rooms in Michigan correctional facilities are lined with vending machines. This is one of several ways that the state makes big dollars in the prison system. Inmates and their guests often gorge themselves on all kinds of hot food, sandwiches, sweets, salty snacks, and soft drinks.

The guard in charge of the visitation room must give an inmate permission to step up to the vending machines. The prisoner's guest may bring in up to twenty dollars worth of quarters.

I should have known better. I'd been priding myself on being such a wonderful friend to Maurice Carter all these years, and I then I forget a simple but very important little matter like food.

I always had only one thing on my mind, and that was the wonderful opportunity to sit next to Maurice and enjoy delightful moments of conversation and laughter. I had smelled the often cloying odors of microwaved burritos, popcorn, and the like, but these aromas did little for *my* appetite. As it turns out, that was very selfish of me. I learned very late in our relationship that Maurice wanted food and, God bless him, he finally told me.

I loaded up with quarters, bringing the maximum amount for our next visit. I suspected that he would probably want a sandwich and a soft drink.

My estimates were short. This man was hungry.

Thereafter, whenever I would visit, I made trip after trip to the vending machines. On a typical visit Maurice would order one steak burger, one cheeseburger, one bag of potato chips, and possibly another of corn chips, one large bottled drink, and finally a dessert, which usually consisted of a cinnamon roll or a slice of pie. I couldn't have eaten that much if I had skipped breakfast and lunch.

He would take his time spreading mustard and mayonnaise on his sandwiches. Then you had to be there to appreciate his first bite into that hamburger. It finally dawned on me after hearing the moans and groans and grunts of approval: Prison food just isn't good. Said Maurice: "This is so much better than the food I get at chow time!"

Looking back, I cannot imagine how I missed all the signs.

I should have remembered that Maurice loved food because the topic came up often in our telephone conversations. Maurice had completed a culinary course while in prison. He had worked on numerous occasions when extra personnel were needed in the kitchen to prepare special banquets. He could create delightful sauces, he claimed, from scratch.

He loved to talk about food with our son-in-law, Jon Hamm. Jon is not only a charter boat captain and superb fisherman, he's a fine chef. Maurice would frequently ask me how Marcia or Jon prepared a certain kind of food, and I would just as frequently assure him that he would get personal samples of all upon his freedom.

I also should have remembered his complaints about prison food.

In fact, for Thanksgiving 2003, the prison menu boasted turkey with all the trimmings and pie for dessert. The actual meal consisted of turkey sausage. And the dessert was a dry piece of cake. I asked him about the lies on the menu. "Those are designed to impress the politicians," was his sardonic reply. "The warden wants to impress the big shots with a printed menu that demonstrates just how well prisoners are fed on the holidays."

On the Fourth of July, 2004, he received a holiday hamburger. It was so dry he could hardly eat it, even with the little packet of mustard that he was given to enhance the flavor.

His favorite terrible food story had its origins in one of the Jackson prison facilities.

Maurice said the chef at Jackson had received a shipment of catfish, and he obviously had never prepared catfish before. There was no way that Maurice was going to take one bite of this entrée when it was presented. He swore that when he went through the chow line, a whole boiled catfish (boiled!), with head still attached, was plopped onto his plate!

FEBRUARY 2004

Dr. Martin Luther King, Jr., once said, "Our lives begin to end the day we become silent about things that matter."

The more we waited for news from the court, the more helpless I felt. I could no longer stifle my thoughts about Judge Hammond.

I'm enough of a realist to know that it's pretty difficult to fight city hall, especially if that city hall is an elected judge. But I would have been remiss if I didn't make some effort to advise the judicial powers that be about His Honor's scurrilous behavior. (This is the man elected to serve the people of Berrien County who, upon seeing the large stack of paper representing four years of legal work on behalf of Maurice Carter, sneered, "Some forest in Canada probably got cut down to make all that paper.")

I drafted a grievance against Judge Hammond and filed it with the State of Michigan's Judicial Tenure Commission on February 4. With the help of several of our attorney friends, I outlined seven complaints against the judge.

I thought one of my strongest arguments was that the judge violated Canon 2 of the Michigan Code of Judicial Conduct, which says that "without regard to a person's race, gender, or other protected personal characteristic, a judge should treat every person fairly, *with courtesy and respect*" [italics mine]. His comment to *Grand Rapids Press* staff writer Pat Shellenbarger, when discussing Maurice Carter's serious illness ("Everybody dies sooner or later anyway.") showed courtesy and respect?

But while filing the complaint may have made me feel better, and may have demonstrated to Maurice that I would come to his defense as if he were a member of my family, it changed nothing and was completely unsuccessful. I received this reply in April: *Because the Commission has determined that there is no basis here for commencing formal disciplinary proceedings or taking any other action, the file in this matter has been closed.*

A feeling of helplessness prodded me into action on another score. It was time to call a summit meeting to discuss ways to make *something* happen! Many of our consultants work in the Chicago area, so I invited some key professionals in the Midwest involved in our case to attend a luncheon meeting on Friday, April 13, 2004.

Those who attended included Professor David Protess, journalism professor and director of the Medill Innocence Project; author Alex Kotlowitz; *Chicago Tribune* columnist Eric Zorn; and *Tribune* investigative reporter Steve Mills.

Some felt that solving the crime was the route to take, even though the Chicago journalists had no interest in covering such a story. I concurred that we should be doing more, especially now that we believed we knew the identity of the shooter.

We didn't solve the world's problems, but Protess came up with an idea regarding statistics that everyone liked, and which ultimately resulted in some fine news coverage. He assigned some of his Innocence Project personnel to check out the average length of a sentence for someone who was convicted of a charge similar to that of Maurice. That turned out to be time-consuming, because every state words its charges a bit differently.

Anyway, one month later his team came up with some good stuff, and a number of reporters pounced on it.

Their data were gathered from the Corrections Unit of the Bureau of Justice Statistics. The Bureau compiled data at the end of the year 2000 on all attempted murder convictions from seventeen states. It chose those seventeen because they happen to house 75 percent of the nation's inmates. The study tracked 11,000 prisoners who had been convicted on some type of attempted murder charge.

The inmates released in 2000 (1,300 of the 11,000 studied) had served an average of eighty-five months behind bars. That's about seven years, or more than twenty years fewer than Maurice had served as of that date.

Of the 11,000 inmates, 33.8 percent had been sentenced to twenty years or longer. Only 1 percent of those who remained in custody in 2000, however, had *actually served* at least twenty years of their sentence. In other words, 99 percent had served fewer than twenty years. A Bureau statistician told the researcher that "only a handful" of the 1 percent had been incarcerated as many years as Maurice had—perhaps as few as one-tenth of 1 percent. That said to me that there is a remote possibility that Maurice Carter had been in prison longer than anyone else in the United States on such a charge.

Updates from 2004 show that, of the current inmates who are incarcerated for this charge, the average time being served is sixty-eight months.

Commented Protess in a statement he gave to the media, "The overwhelming evidence of [Maurice's] innocence makes this problem all the more outrageous."

The system remained stubbornly motionless.

From the time Maurice's liver disease was openly revealed in mid–2003, doctors speculated on how long Maurice Carter could live without a liver transplant. Some were not all that optimistic, saying that, if Maurice suffered a severe setback, he could die at any time.

You'll sense my uneasiness in this report, sent out on the Maurice Carter e-mail information network on Sunday, February 22, 2004:

> Maurice Carter and I have an agreement. He will call me from prison every week, usually on two different days, but always at least once. Now that he has been diagnosed with liver disease (end stage) and Parkinson's disease, this communication is more important than ever.
>
> When I did not receive a call from the prison on Thursday, and when no call came on Friday or Saturday either, I made a beeline for the prison on Sunday.
>
> I recognized instantly that Maurice's condition had deteriorated. I could tell by his appearance, gait, speech, and sluggish memory. I explained that the absence of telephone calls mandated a visit. He attributed the lack of telephone calls to a "little relapse."
>
> While the legal process plods along, while the prosecutor's office continues to oppose our every move, while a crooked defense attorney tries to persuade another inmate to claim that Maurice confessed to the crime, while a smug judge stands by his refusal to grant a new trial with the words "we all have to die sometime," while physicians argue about whether Maurice has six months or twelve months to live, and while a hesitant governor seems to want still one more medical report to justify commuting an unfair and unjust sentence, the condition of Maurice Carter worsens!
>
> I had 45 minutes before the visiting period ended … 45 minutes to build up his spirits and give him new hope.

Because of his memory lapse, I did some name-dropping to remind him of the high level of support he enjoys. I bought him a hamburger from a vending machine and you would have thought it was a filet mignon. He relished the taste of his Diet Pepsi as if it were a bottle of fine wine. And I concluded the short visit by retelling the story of a giant billboard truck that will head for the State Capitol. He marveled when I described the size of the sign that will call on Governor Granholm to show compassion.

My efforts paid off!

When a stern guard advised us that visiting hours were over and all visitors were instructed to leave, we hugged.

As I walked out of the visiting room, he smiled.

I wept.

> … *The GOD ON THE MOUNTAIN is still God in the valley.*
> *When things go wrong, He'll make them right.*
> *And the God in the good times is still God in the bad times.*
> *The God of the day is still God of the night.*[29]

It was February 23, the date for the regular monthly meeting of the Citizens Committee for the Release of Maurice Carter. I wondered if anyone would attend. Scott Elliott, our chairman, had forgotten to send out the notices. He, like the rest of us, had been trying to carry more hay than his fork could handle. In addition, he was struggling with some health problems.

Lisa Connell, Scott Elliott, and I huddled around the table in our little meeting room in downtown Benton Harbor. Then Joyce Gouwens showed up. Joyce is the wife of a retired Presbyterian minister, a fine musician, a social activist with a heart of gold, and a staunch supporter of efforts to free Maurice Carter.

As I began the meeting with a review of my recent Chicago meeting, I was interrupted by the entrance of two strangers.

"Oh, Hi Mavis. Thank you for coming." Joyce Gouwens welcomed the young white woman. "This is Lateesha," said Mavis, introducing us to her African-American friend. Then Mavis explained, "We both have spent time in prison, and we decided we wanted to come and find out more about this committee. We've been reading about Maurice Carter in the newspaper, and it sounds like he got a raw deal."

I tried to restart my report to the committee, but it wasn't easy. Mavis was a talker and frequently interrupted to tell about her experiences with the justice system in Berrien County and her experiences behind bars. Lateesha, on the other hand, remained silent throughout my presentation.

Wondering how much I dared say about the Billy Lee Brown situation, I decided to go with it. I reminded our committee members that we believed we had established the identity of the shooter but had exhausted all efforts to get beyond that. Aaron McFee (my friend Dawg) was good enough to come forward with the story, but refused to let us talk with his mother, or to go with any of our teams to Ohio to confront his uncle in person. So, we were at a standstill. There was general agreement among all of our legal consultants that, if we solved the crime, Maurice would go free.

Finally Lateesha spoke up. First she wanted to know if the man named Dawg was the same Dawg with whom she was acquainted. Then she wanted to know if his mom lived on London Avenue. Directing the questions to me, she quickly realized that I knew the names of the main characters of this story and that we were talking about the same people. In fact, her baby girl was being cared for by Dawg's mother while Lateesha attended this meeting.

She stated that she was a Christian, that she didn't think it was right that an innocent man was in prison, and that she would help where she could.

Not wanting to get my hopes too high, I said that I would speak with her in private following the meeting.

Lateesha and I started comparing notes. I told her everything that Dawg had told me, and she reaffirmed her commitment to help us. We exchanged e-mail addresses and parted ways.

I had private doubts that anything profitable would come from this committee meeting. It turned out to be one of the most significant of all meetings.

After listening to Lateesha, Scott Elliott shook his head in disbelief. "There must be dozens of people who know who shot Tom Schadler."

Some days the trip home took forever. It went quickly this time.

Tuesday morning I was still pinching myself, disbelieving that we were getting a break. By midday I could take it no longer. Using the excuse that perhaps I hadn't written down her e-mail address correctly, I sent a brief message to Lateesha. Her reply: "they tol me a lil about it and who really did to the shooting. i really don't want to say this over the e-mail." She promised to call me that night.

No call.

Is the roller coaster going up or down?

I awoke Wednesday morning after a restless night. And then came the telephone call I was waiting for.

Billy Lee Brown was our man. Lateesha claimed she found a "crack head" who not only confirmed this, but said he knew why Billy Lee did it. But there was another snag. The guy was scared to death of Billy Lee. We would encounter that snag time and again. The drug addict said he wanted to "be careful,

didn't want nobody to come after him." Based on information I had accumulated already and would accumulate in the
future, I think just about everyone in the 'hood was afraid of
Billy Lee. He was said to be the center of attention when he
snuck into town, but the general consensus was that he was
a big, mean, drunken bully. And, as Dawg told me, he liked
to fight.

Lateesha turned out to be determined and fearless, daring
to ask numerous people in the McFee family about Billy Lee
Brown. That worried me for two reasons. One, I was afraid
someone would get suspicious and do something to her. And,
two, we were not getting this stuff documented. If we went
back later to try to record this, these people might be reluctant to discuss it a second time. But, as Maurice and I said so
often, we had to leave it in God's hands … the same God that
Lateesha loved and worshiped and the same God who would
protect her during this touchy situation.

And what information she garnered!

Lateesha talked to Dawg's grandmother, who reportedly allowed Billy Lee to take refuge in her home after the crime,
until they could collect the money to ship him off to Ohio.
She readily admitted that Billy Lee did it.

"Dawg's grannie said that when billy lee shot the police
that he come to her house and said I got that m___f___ and
said nobody got to worry about him also she told me that he
had to stay clear of the streets and he stayed at her house in
till they got the money… ."

Lateesha talked to Dawg's mother, who also knew the
whole story.

I believe Scott Elliott was correct. Dozens of people in the
inner city knew who committed the crime.

Down goes the roller coaster! Lisa Connell called. Maurice was rushed back to Duane Waters Hospital the previous night.

I knew his ammonia level had been getting too high again. Even in the C Unit, right next door to the hospital, staffers were not paying attention to his medication and diet needs. Maurice (who was also diabetic) said that one guard told him he couldn't have his special diet any more. A nurse informed the guard that he didn't have the authority to make that decision. The guard replied to "just watch him." Sure enough, Maurice didn't get his special diet after that.

Mary Blackwell checked with a nurse at the hospital, and learned Maurice was doing much better. Of course he was. He was at last getting appropriate care. How difficult was that to understand?

Later in the day I spoke with Scott Morgan, the medical social worker, and the roller coaster dipped a little lower. Maurice was in Duane Waters for good. He was deemed to be so fragile that they could not take any more chances by placing him in other facilities. He would die in that hell hole unless we got him out. Nothing was happening in the courts. It was time for the governor to take action.

FIFTEEN

MARCH 2004

I purchased a miniature digital recorder for Lateesha. She made a trial run with the recorder, and the unit's microphone didn't pick up the voices of other people. The recorder had to be returned to the store and replaced with a tiny tape recorder. A simple project for you or me, but amazingly complex when you consider that Lateesha had no money and the store was eighty miles away.

And so this didn't happen in hours, or even days. It took a lot of days. But we finally got a new recorder that seemed to fill the bill, could be easily hidden, and had good reproduction quality.

Professor Protess gave me specific instructions on the questions that Lateesha should ask members of the family so that, if recordings were made, we not only had the information we wanted, but we also had the name of the person being interviewed and the date. I reviewed the instructions with this courageous young woman, and she did an amazing job!

Consider this: Here's a young single mother from the inner city who has had a most difficult life, but who places her trust in God and who believes that if Maurice didn't get a fair shake, it's her responsibility to do something about it. And so she wears a wire. She tucks away a miniature recorder, placing the microphone in her bra. Then she walks right into the heart of the 'hood to discuss the shooting of Tom Schadler with her own friends and family and acquaintances. This is a subject that has been taboo since 1973. The risks were huge. Just one slipup and she would be ostracized by her immediate family and her closest friends forever. God blessed her efforts.

Interview One: With Mama Nana

L: Hey, Mama Nana.

MN: Huh, how're you doin'?

L: Can I ask you something?

MN: Yeah

L: I know you're tired of me asking but, uh, what happened when Uncle Billy Lee shot the, uh, police Schadler? What did he say?

MN: He glad he shot that racist m____f____. He fired the gun and bust out laughin'.

L: Whatcha y'all do?

MN: Looked at him like he was crazy. Said, "Boy you ain't did nothin' like that. We know you ain't did nothin' like that!"

L: And what did he say?

MN: "I did do it!"

L: And what, uh, Billy Lee say?

MN: (inaudible) … admit that he did it.

L: And how did, and then what happened? How did he end up in Ohio?

MN: His mom got scared and sent him to Ohio.

L: Oh. Who else know Billy Lee shot him?

MN: Huh?

L: … shot the police Schadler?

MN: (inaudible) … Melika knows. [A relative]

L: Why he want to shoot him?

MN: Cause he said he was a racist. He didn't like black people.

L: Did he ever arrest Uncle Billy Lee?

MN: He had got, last I heard, he had got on Billy Lee for something.

L: You can't remember what for?

MN: Uh-uh. It's been so long ago.

L: So where is Billy Lee now?

MN: He's still in Ohio last time I heard.

L: He don't, you don't never hear from him?

MN: No. You're kin with his family.

L: I wish I could get in touch with him.

MN: I don't know nobody around here got that address.

L: Oh. A lot of people know he shot, um, that police.

L: [re: Maurice] They say he gonna die.

MN: How you know all of this?

L: I read it on a paper.

MN: You ain't talking to the folks that, that Dawg is talk to, is you?

L: No. Who Dawg talkin' to?

MN: I don't know, supposed to be some people that tryin' to find out your cousin Billy did it.

L: He still be talking to 'em?

MN: I haven't seen Dawg in three days. I guess he still is.

Bingo! And that wasn't the only recording. That gutsy Lateesha went right after Dawg's mother, and then Dawg's uncle. I was in Madison, Wisconsin, meeting with Keith Findley and the Innocence Project team when Lisa called with the good news. The tapes had clarity, and they were safely in our hands!

Interview Two: With Dawg's mother, Hattie

H: What, girl?

L: Do you remember, uh, when that cop shot, when the officer, Schadler, got shot? Did Billy Lee do that?

H: Now what you ask me that for? You tryin' to figure out some stuff? What you ask me that now? That stuff happened so long ago. Girl, I can't even remember what all happened. But I know he did it. I know he did it!

L: Did you know, uh, the man, Maurice Carter?

H: Nah, I didn't. I, I didn't know him. I did not know him. You know the same questions you askin' me, Dawg asked me, too. What's wrong with y'all? Dawg had some white man up in my house trying to get information for that white man. I told Dawg he better leave that shit alone. Now here you come. Is you workin' for them people, too?

L: No, why y'all keep askin' me that?

H: 'Cause you askin' the same questions. Billy Lee shot that policeman. Everybody know it. The white folks know it. The police know it! They just ain't doin' shit about it! Now don't ask me nothin' else.

I think Scott Elliott underestimated the number of people who knew who really shot Tom Schadler! The next interview is with Dawg's Uncle.

Interview Three: With Dawg's Uncle Pops

L: Let me ask you somethin'. Remember when that police officer, Schadler, got shot? What, what, what really happened? Why did, why did Uncle Billy Lee shoot him?

P: Why are ... what is it you keep asking me that question for, girl? I, I told you, girl, the man is crazy. He's done shot more than just Officer Schadler. I don't even know if that's the man name. It happened so long ago ... Billy Lee, Billy Lee, he shot that man, sure did! And, and, and Mama and everybody else know he did it. Mama done helped him get out of town.

L: Why they help him get out of town if he shot that man? He shouldn't have ... they shouldn't have did that. They just more involved in it than he.

P: Well don't nobody [inaudible] talk about it. I don't like talking about it. Just don't like talking about it. 'Cause, cause Billy Lee, I don't want him gettin' mad at me if anything goin' on about that junk. 'Cause, see Dawg had a whole bunch stuff goin' on. Dawg got riled up in some stuff and, and, and that doggone Dawg got riled up in some stuff trying to find out who did what and, and, and had them folks all in his mother's house. He was even drivin' a white man's car. They tell me, I, I don't know. But I know, I know Billy Lee did it. He sure did. I was, I was, I was over Mama's house on Meadow.

We'll never know how many lives Maurice has touched. I received an e-mail message from a woman I'll call Michelle. I have no idea how she obtained my e-mail address. I know that she's a Christian because she said so.

The message was short. A nurse at Duane L. Waters Hospital, she could be in trouble for contacting me. She wanted me to know that Maurice Carter had touched her life. She said that she had read his story and wondered if there was anything that she could do for him.

These few words contained a huge gift. I asked her to keep an eye on him, keep him comfortable, demonstrate kindness, and show God's love.

Thank you, Lord, for this dear woman. We see you in her!

Governor Granholm continued to delay while Maurice's health continued to fail. She needed a prod.

My nephew Tom Kuiper owns a little advertising agency. He started out by selling advertising signs in public restroom stalls, hence the name of his company, Captive Audience Advertising. The growing company has had great success, and recently Tom decided to expand into other areas. He purchased a used billboard truck. Instead of people looking at billboards along the highways, he decided to bring the billboard to the people. We're not talking about a miniature billboard here. This billboard is 12-by-20 feet. Actually there are two of them, mounted on the back of a specially-designed truck, facing opposite directions. At the base of the billboards are floodlights.

This young entrepreneur was very interested in my new organization called INNOCENT!. He explained that he was in no position to support us financially, but he had an idea. He would be willing to donate the use of the billboard truck. As we talked our ideas solidified into a billboard to apply pressure on the governor.

I provided the copy: "Governor Granholm: SHOW COM-
PASSION! Commute the sentence of Carter." Tom's graphic
artist did magnificent work. The background was white; most
of the words were in gray. The words "SHOW COMPAS-
SION" and "Carter" were in red. Alongside the words they
reproduced a full-color closeup photograph of Maurice Carter's face.

We launched the billboard truck on its maiden voyage. Tom
drove it to a watering hole where a number of Studebaker
drivers gather each Saturday noon to enjoy Studeburgers,
suds, and stories. To say that the truck caused a commotion
would be putting it mildly.

By that time I had faxed all the media, alerting them to the
fact that the truck would be heading for Lansing the following Thursday, March 18.

We milked that story for all it was worth.

We started Thursday morning with a press conference in our
hometown, Grand Haven, Michigan. Waiting until Thursday
always makes good sense. Municipal, county and education
meetings are usually held Mondays, Tuesdays, and Wednesdays,
and the news people are busy. By Thursday, they're sniffing for
something interesting.

Then on to Grand Rapids for a second press conference,
this in Michigan's second largest city, home of many major
media including three commercial television stations.

Both press conferences brought the desired results. Did I
mention that it was cold and windy with a slight drizzle? This
was becoming all too typical for a Carter event.

Finally, we aimed the truck toward Lansing. Tom and I
learned that you don't drive a towering billboard truck very
fast on the open highway, even when traffic is light, and especially if there are high winds. It's like steering a sailboat down
the expressway, only not quite as thrilling.

The maiden voyage of our billboard truck
on Thursday, March 18, 2004

Our dear friend and staunch supporter Dena Anderson, sometime guest writer for the *Lansing State Journal*, had rented parking meters for us at a most strategic location. We parked the billboard truck so that one sign faced one of the entrances to the State Capitol. The sign on the other side of the truck faced Governor Granholm's office. We were parked just a stone's throw from her window.

Tom snapped an amazing picture of the truck with the Capitol dome in the background that he used later for promotional purposes. I quickly made an 8 x 10 print and sent it to Maurice. Later that day came the television news footage and the front page pictures in newspapers.

Despite a traffic jam (the perfect place for a billboard truck), Tom and I made it home in time for Maurice's regular call.

Did I have good news for him: first, the success of our friend Lateesha in secretly recording the revealing conversations; and then the story of Tom and Doug and the billboard truck. He chortled throughout my rundown of all the events of that memorable day. If the mobile billboard project did nothing more than buoy his spirits, it was worth the effort.

> *Go, tell it on the mountains,*
> *Over the hills and everywhere.* [30]

The *South Bend Tribune*, sparked on by our message to the governor, contacted her press secretary. Governor Granholm delivered a prepared statement for the media: "We're looking at the totality of circumstances included in Maurice Carter's file to determine whether, if he is released, he will present a danger to the community."

Can you believe that?

Chicago Tribune columnist Eric Zorn couldn't. He printed a sarcastic little item on his website, entitled "The Appalling Coward Who Sits in the Governor's Office in Michigan."

Said Zorn, in response to the prepared statement: "The man is 60 years old, dying of liver disease in a prison hospital and has no record of criminal violence other than a dismaying conviction on shockingly weak evidence of an attempted murder that happened more than 30 years ago.

"This gravely ill man has served more than four times the average sentence for attempted murder despite the outrageous shabbiness of the case against him, and Granholm is dithering about whether he's 'a danger to the community.'

"I used to think of this as Blagojevich Syndrome—named after our (Illinois) Gov. Rod, who seems to fear more than anything being labeled soft on crime, a particular affliction of moderate Democrats—but I may have to rename it Granholm's Disease." [31]

I posted the following e-mail message to our supporters:

There'll be a birthday party for Maurice Carter next Monday evening, complete with a cake and candles! Will Maurice receive just songs and cards as he turns 60, or will he receive the gift of a lifetime, freedom?

The bigger questions are these: Will Michigan Governor Jennifer Granholm, a former prosecutor and former Attorney General, stick with her prosecutor mentality and decide that a jury has spoken (even though it never heard the facts of the case), and that a judge was within his rights to hand down a life sentence (even though the Berrien County Good Ol' Boy System saw to it that Maurice was never granted parole) on the charge of assault with intent to murder, and that misinformation about his prison record need not be verified?

Or will she demonstrate some real compassion and grit of state leadership, supported by new statistics from the Bureau of Justice and a new medical report from a leading hepatologist? Will she personally make the short drive to Duane L. Waters Hospital in Jackson (39 miles) next Monday? Will she be processed and frisked at the hospital doors, will she wait on one of the steel benches (without backs) that the state so graciously provides for patients and visitors, will she look into the eyes of the kind and gentle man who has already served four times longer than almost anyone else in the country for such a crime (even though he is innocent), will she personally shake the hand of this critically ill patient dying of liver disease, will she be impressed by his undying faith, and will she present him with a *real* birthday gift, a sentence commutation, *the gift of life?*

All eyes are on the governor.

The conversation with Maurice on the evening of Saturday, March 28 was rather somber. I am carefully describing the conversation because my guts were churning; my blood pressure was going up. Perhaps you're one of those people who think prisoners don't deserve humane treatment. Maurice didn't mean to be stirring up my emotions as he talked, but two little things that he mentioned in passing nearly sent me into orbit.

Number one, this is still the month of March, generally a chilly month in the Michigan weather pattern. Today, only God knows why, the officials in charge at the Duane L. Waters Hospital decided to turn on the air conditioning. Maurice thought that perhaps the medical people wanted to purify the air. From his account, I learned that purification of the air may have been accomplished, but the inmates were freezing. The little radiator designed to deliver heat in his hospital room was losing its battle with the air conditioner. He was cold.

Number two, allegedly because of prison budget problems, there weren't enough clean clothes for the inmates. That may not have bothered every inmate in that hospital, but it bothered Maurice Carter, who has always been especially sensitive about cleanliness and personal hygiene. This critically ill hospital patient had to resort to washing his own garments. He was allowed to use the laundry facilities for white items such as underwear. For anything with color, like the standard prison-issue apparel, he was doing his laundry right there in his hospital room using shampoo.

There is a balm in Gilead to make the wounded whole,
There is a balm in Gilead to heal the sin-sick soul.[32]

March 29 was approaching. No word from the governor. The day arrived. Still no word from the governor. My message on the evening of March 29 to our supporters on the network:

How do you wish "happy birthday" to the kindest, most gentle, wrongly convicted inmate in the Michigan prison system? With tears, that's how.

In my 7-year friendship with Maurice Carter, this was perhaps the most poignant moment!

Professor Keith Findley, co-director of the University of Wisconsin Innocence Project, and one of the I.P. law students, accepted the collect call from Maurice Carter promptly at 7 p.m. tonight. Keith, in turn, dialed the Benton Harbor telephone number where eight members of the Citizens Committee for the Release of Maurice Carter were crowded into the tiny office of committee chair Scott Elliott.

One by one, the people in Wisconsin and in Michigan introduced themselves and wished Maurice a happy 60th. With a voice weakened by the ravages of end-stage hepatitis C, Maurice Carter thanked all for their work, and especially for helping to keep his spirits alive.

Maurice Carter's 60th birthday party, sans Maurice

After all had spoken, the entire group of Wisconsin and Michigan participants sang "Happy Birthday."

The 15-minute telephone "party" was ended with expressions of love.

I went on in detail about the Benton Harbor birthday party. We offered a mimosa toast and faked frivolity as we nibbled at ice cream and cake. We took pictures for Maurice, but it wasn't right. He wasn't there.

How do you react when you realize that Maurice Carter's birthday has come and gone, and the Governor of Michigan has missed a golden opportunity to commute the sentence of your brother, your hero?

With tears, that's how.

April 2004

No regular call from Maurice on April 11. More worry.

A quick check with medical social worker Scott Morgan on April 12 confirmed my fears. Maurice's ammonia level was way up. An IV had been started.

Maurice and I resumed communication on April 18 via telephone. This time, in addition to his kindness, weakness could be detected in his voice.

Because nothing was happening on the other key issue, exposing the real criminal in the Tom Schadler shooting, I continued to push for and finally received approval to turn over the Lateesha tapes to Pat Shellenbarger. This was a major step that ultimately led to some interesting experiences for both Shellenbarger and me. More about that later.

On April 19, our Michigan attorney Gary Giguere passed along some bad news from Grand Rapids. The Michigan Court of Appeals had turned us down by a vote of two to one. The next step was the Michigan Supreme Court, a conservative court that has yet to demonstrate any compassion for the little guy.

At that point, you might assume that the roller coaster is running on pretty low tracks, right? Then hang on, because Governor Granholm must have been waiting for that decision by the Court of Appeals.

One day later, April 20, Maurice's cousin Mary Blackwell received an early morning call from Scott Morgan at
the hospital, telling her that Maurice would have a parole
board hearing the next morning at the hospital! What the
heck? This very board had voted against a medical commutation several months before. Morgan commented that this was
most unusual. As we say in the news business, sources who
insisted on anonymity indicated that this came straight from
the governor. Carter supporters were surprised to receive a
message from me that day that didn't sound like my usual self.
I wanted everyone to refrain from putting pressure on the
governor's office until this hearing was over. There was to be
no rocking of the boat at this critical juncture.

I visited Maurice in the hospital later that same day. The
latest developments had given this ill and weak man new hope.
The hearing was scheduled for nine o'clock the next morning right at the hospital, and the person scheduled to conduct
the hearing was none other than the chair of the Michigan
Parole Board, John Rubitschun. Maurice was allowed an advocate in the hearing. He chose me to be at his side.

While I continued to feel an intimate kinship with Maurice, thinking about the impact of my words at the hearing
the next morning began to overwhelm me. My words would
seriously influence his future.

Attorney Gary Giguere began coaching me on what to say,
emphasizing that I stick to health issues because the parole
board does not decide innocence or guilt. Rather, it assumes
guilt. The board had been instructed to make a recommendation to Governor Granholm on the question of commuting
the Carter sentence solely for medical reasons.

I began praying that God would give me the right words.
Before retiring that night, I went to the computer and worked
on an outline. It was a short night. I was up at four o'clock

the next morning. I had been in Jackson to visit Maurice in the hospital the day before, and had been instructed to arrive for the hearing by eight o'clock. Scott Morgan was very kind when he welcomed me. Rubitschun arrived moments later, and he was all business. He quickly briefed me as to how the hearing would be conducted. It would be strictly an interview between Rubitschun and Maurice. I was not to participate, and I should not interject any comments. At the conclusion of the interview I would be given an opportunity to speak and, while he didn't want me talking all morning, he gave me no specific time constraints. Again came instructions that I must stick to the subject: health issues. Any comments about the case, about crime, about Maurice's innocence, were forbidden. "I believe he's guilty," said Rubitschun.

I was not intimidated. "I believe he's innocent," I replied calmly.

We were ushered into a small examining room and encouraged to sit on anything handy, including an examination table. In addition to Rubitschun, Maurice, and myself, two other hospital staff members were present: counselor Marilyn Shears and Scott Morgan. Their presence was important, because the parole board needed experts to testify as to the seriousness of Maurice's health setbacks and to the fact that he did not have any dangerous personality characteristics.

Maurice was late because the governor had ordered a last-minute physical examination. When he finally shuffled in, obviously ill and clad in pajamas, the doctor gave a quick verbal report to Rubitschun that the patient was OK for the moment. No dramatic changes.

Maurice was directed to a chair directly across from Rubitschun. I had suggested, and Scott Morgan had agreed, that we deliver him to the hearing in a wheelchair. Maurice wanted no part of that. He was going to *walk* through that door. No one ever accused him of not being strong-willed.

He may have walked slowly, but his mind was keen. He may have been poorly dressed, but he carried himself with dignity. He must have lost his nice pair of eyeglasses, because he was wearing a set of prison issue glasses that were too large. His head appeared even smaller, now that he had lost so much weight. That morning, my heart melted for him.

This may have been one of our finest hours. We worked as a team, and God gets the glory.

There were some things that baffled me about the hearing. We were warned in advance to stick with health issues, but when the hearing began, the man presiding, a former prosecutor, behaved as if he were a prosecutor again. First he reviewed Carter's arrest record prior to the crime in 1973 (What did this have to do with his health?) He concluded that part of the discussion with this snide remark: "It's no surprise to me that you ended up in prison."

The next phase of the interview focused on Maurice's behavior while in prison, and more specifically on a stabbing incident. Maurice readily admitted that he had injured another inmate, explaining that it was in self-defense. The guy, a bodybuilder and weightlifter, had made threats against Maurice, and Maurice had been afraid. Maurice went on to explain that this dangerous prisoner was later transferred to another prison, where he stabbed a guard. As an afterthought he added, "I apologized to the man afterwards for what had happened." Typical Maurice.

After that we got down to a more sensible discussion: where he would work, where he would live, whether he could get appropriate medical treatment, and so forth.

Then it was my turn.

I gave a character reference, explained that we would work with Maurice's family on appropriate housing accommodations and appropriate medical care. I begged for expediency, producing a recent letter from the University of Wisconsin School of Medicine stating that Maurice could die during one of his high-ammonia-level episodes. I assured the parole board that Maurice would have gainful employment after he received a new liver.

Finally, Rubitschun threw his curve ball at Maurice. "If I told you that I had a piece of paper in my pocket that would allow you to walk out of here with Mr. Tjapkes right now, as a free man, if you would just confess to this crime, what would you say?"

Quietly: "I would never confess to something that I didn't do."

Silence. The two parties locked eyes, and Maurice did not waver.

The hearing was over. The uncomfortable moment had passed.

Maurice, ever the master at public relations, thanked the chairman of the parole board for the manner in which he had conducted this interview.

I was granted permission to give Maurice a hug, and we were then directed to part ways. For the second consecutive day I left him with tears in my eyes.

Down the elevator, down the stairs, through the lobby … my thoughts were whirling as I walked through the parking lot to my car. Had I used the right words? I asked God to bless the words of two imperfect human beings.

"Mr. Tjapkes!"

I wheeled around. John Rubitschun was approaching me. He wanted to talk some more. I had only Maurice's freedom on my mind. Before he started talking I gave him some praise, explaining that I was a former reporter and was able to recognize a good prosecutor. Emulating Maurice's PR skills, I then thanked him for treating Maurice like a human being, even though they gently agreed to disagree. He responded with a slight smile.

Rubitschun went on to explain the process as it might play out. The board meeting was scheduled for that Friday, two days away. If the board voted in favor of recommending a commutation ("I know how I intend to vote. I can't speak for the rest of the board," he said.), a public hearing must be held in sixty days. He seemed worried about a giant public demonstration, something that he knew very well we could generate. He said that the hearing would be held right there at the hospital in a meeting room. I could produce as many witnesses as I wished, but he wanted the subject matter restricted to character references, and he wanted the length of the testimony from each person tightly restricted.

I assured him that those of us who supported Maurice Carter could and would abide by his wishes.

We parted on friendly terms, calling each other by first names, and I felt a new confidence that we would get a favorable vote by members of the parole board.

It was late morning when I steered my way out of the prison complex. I felt like I had already worked a full day.

Early Friday morning, the day that the parole board decision was expected, Marcia and I were winging our way to Austin, Texas. I had hoped that Maurice would be able to accompany us this year to the annual national conference of the Innocence Network. All of the organizations that work on behalf of the wrongly convicted are represented at these conferences, and the guests of honor are those who have been exonerated. Maurice deserved to be here this year, telling his story, receiving accolades, basking in the sunlight of freedom.

I kept the cell phone nearby.

The call came early in the afternoon, Texas time. Unanimous vote in favor of Maurice, 9 to 0! Praise God! Just to clarify, this vote was strictly on the issue of whether to hold a public hearing. Before plans were made, however, the Berrien County Prosecutor and Berrien County Circuit Court Judge John Hammond had thirty days to express their feelings about such a hearing. If they had no objections, the hearing would be held about thirty days thereafter. The parole board would make its final recommendation to the governor after the public hearing. The governor then had a period of time to act on the parole board recommendation. Even then, there would be a built-in delay if she granted the commutation. If the ailing Maurice could survive all of that it would be a miracle.

But, for now, celebration time. The roller coaster is soaring! At times like this it feels pretty heady to be the center of attention. The calls from the media poured in as the word spread. I loved being Maurice's spokesman. Not wishing to make any waves, I praised the parole board and urged everyone to speed up the process.

I was able to persuade some key players in the Carter defense team to hold a brief strategy session while in Texas. We pulled together the codirectors of the Wisconsin project, Keith Findley and John Pray, as well as Rob Warden and Larry Marshall from Northwestern University Law School's Center on Wrongful Convictions. I wanted to make sure that everyone was comfortable with revealing the Lateesha tapes to Pat Shellenbarger of *The Grand Rapids Press*, as we seemed to be making little progress in the Billy Lee Brown investigation. Not only general agreement, but widespread enthusiasm permeated our short meeting in a hotel corridor. I would carry out my assignment to work with Shellenbarger upon our return to Michigan.

At the conclusion of the conference Marcia and I rented a car and found the highway to the city of Livingston. I had an appointment to visit a client of INNOCENT! who was on death row. We drove in a pounding rain storm for one hour, windshield wipers at high speed, worming our way through construction projects, all the while trying to read highway signs, and my mumbling all kinds of unpleasant words and phrases. Marcia remained quiet.

There wasn't much to Livingston, Texas, except some of the finest barbecue I've ever tasted at a place called Bodacious Barbecue. We checked into a motel along the highway. I struck up a conversation with the nice young woman at the desk, whose accent was pure Texas. Somehow in our discussion I alerted her to the fact that I would be wearing a clerical collar, my standard uniform for prison visits. That plus the clergy card make for a smooth path behind bars.

Now tell me that God doesn't have a plan. She was in the process of writing a letter to her brother—you guessed it—in prison.

I went back to the room, decided that a little libation was in order after such a terrible day on the highway, and the room telephone rang. That was unusual, because no one knew where we were staying. It was the woman at the front desk.

"Will you do me a favor? Will you pray for my brother?"

I remembered that I had taken a few of the Al Hoksbergen devotional booklets along for the Innocence Conference. I retrieved one from the car and gave it to her.

I love visiting with prisoners, but I hate going to prisons.

I had made advance arrangements with a prison chaplain to visit with Charles Anthony Nealy, a resident on death row in the Polunsky Unit. The case was a scam. One Texas newspaper crowed that his was the shortest death penalty trial in history. And they're proud of this stuff? A poor black man, falsely accused, wrongly convicted, now sitting on death row, and remaining there for years as the appeal process creeps along. Even though he enjoys little if any support from family members, he has a pretty decent support network around the world. I was first contacted by someone in England, and I was trying to persuade AIDWYC to jump aboard.

Injustice anywhere is a threat to justice everywhere! [33]

"I don't want you to spend too much money on food, man. These prices are terrible."

I informed Mr. Nealy, who prefers to go by the name Anthony, that I didn't bring in $20 worth of quarters just to take them out again. We were speaking by telephone with bulletproof glass between us. Visitors on death row do not get the luxury of contact visits. No hugs, not even the shaking of hands.

I took his order, astonished that there was someone who could eat more than Maurice. The young woman who served as the guard on duty instructed me to insert the quarters in the huge bank of vending machines, but she would have to touch the food packages. I guess they worry about someone slipping contraband into the food bags. I dutifully pumped the quarters into the slots, doing my part to enrich the Texas Department of Corrections coffers. Out came a submarine sandwich with three meats, a roast beef and cheese sandwich, two bags of different kinds of potato chips, a large bottle of Gatorade, a sweet roll, and a slice of cheesecake. For Anthony, it was a touch of heaven. An hour and a half later, as we bade our farewells, he was tossing away the final scraps of food wrappings.

A well dressed and pleasant woman who I assumed to be some kind of social worker was walking by as I made my exit. I asked for help finding my way out of there. When we approached the front gate she exchanged pleasantries with a guard who appeared to be going off duty. Turns out the pleasantries were one-sided. She asked him how he was doing. He replied that he was doing much better now. He had just resigned. She asked him where in the correctional system he had been working. Second shift, death row. He turned in his badge and walked away.

"Is he serious?" I asked the pretty lady. "Oh yes," she replied. "It happens all the time."

MAY 2004

"It sounds like the people are playacting!"

Disbelief dripped from the lips of Berrien County Prosecutor James Cherry as he listened to a tape of the secretly recorded interviews conducted by Lateesha.

Pat Shellenbarger had managed to get a private audience on May 3 with the prosecutor and his chief investigator, but the atmosphere was one of hostility.

"I find it frankly irritating that this comes up at this point after several appeals. I guess I'm skeptical about this."

Cherry stalked out of the room.

As Pat left the office, he noticed that Mrs. Schadler was sitting in the lobby. Had she overheard the tape? Had she been invited to sit there? Did this prosecutor have one ounce of integrity?

That wasn't Pat's only uncomfortable moment that day.

He drove to Benton Harbor with the hope of meeting still another family member who had overheard Billy Lee Brown at a drinking party boasting about shooting Schadler. Lateesha had warned me, however, that Pat was getting set up to be robbed. I cautioned Pat to be careful when arranging any clandestine meetings.

He took my advice and picked up our committee chairman Scott Elliott first, thinking that two bodies would be better than one. They were scheduled to meet at the home of

Mama Nana, but made a few preliminary passes up and down the street to see if the desired witnesses might have shown up there. The guys finally parked, walked onto the front porch, and knocked on the door. Mama Nana was home and, unaware of the secret recordings, wasn't about to tell anything. Then, a young man they believed was Mama Nana's son approached on crutches and ordered the pair to leave. Ever the reporter, Pat continued to ask questions as the man on the crutches became more belligerent. He threatened that he had some "brothers" who would take care of them if they didn't leave his mother alone. At that point, Pat noticed a group of young guys who had been playing basketball across the street. They were no longer playing basketball. They were in a huddle, intently watching the activity on Mama Nana's front porch. Pat told me that he and Scott felt that it was definitely time to leave.

Pat wanted to talk with Matty, Dawg's drunken uncle who had told me that he had seen Billy Lee run from the scene of the crime. I assured Pat that I would accompany him to Benton Harbor the next time. I thought I could identify Matty.

The next time arrived on May 21, and our first meeting of the day was with Lateesha. Pat's travels in putting together this exposé about Billy Lee were fraught with rough roads and roadblocks. This morning Lateesha still refused to let him use her name in the article but agreed that he could use the contents of the tapes, a significant victory.

We met until almost noon, bought some lunch for Lateesha who we knew was very poor. A free meal for her was a real gift. I left my car at Burger King and climbed into the passenger's seat of Pat's minivan. He knew of a place where drunks hang out along the St. Joseph River, and he wanted to look there for Matty. I was of the opinion that Matty never left the party store parking lot where I last saw him a year ago, but we headed for the river.

I looked to the west, out over Lake Michigan, and muttered to Pat that there would be no drunks in this park today. A storm was obviously moving in. We decided to eat lunch while the storm played itself out, and then we would return to our agenda. He had a list of people he wanted to see, hoping that this would be his last trip to Benton Harbor before publication of the article. We drove to the Ideal Place, a fine little restaurant downtown. As we alit from the vehicle the storm hit with a vengeance.

The strong winds and I had a tug of war as I attempted to close the front door of the restaurant. The face of the eatery was solid glass, so we chose to watch the approaching storm before eating. Tree branches and debris were blowing through an empty lot across the street. Large pieces of sheeting that made up the roof of a nearby vacant factory were torn off by the wind and crashed into the street. Sparks were showering down from broken power lines. Someone in the restaurant screamed. Claiming that we had a tornado on our hands, the owner ran through the dining room, shooing all patrons down a stairway into the basement. Pat and I chose to remain at the window, where the weatherman continued his amazing display. We had gale-force winds, but saw nothing circular. There was no tornado. Pat's minivan appeared to be jumping up and down, and the water in the street was so deep that it was flowing over the curb. We learned later that winds were clocked at ninety-nine miles per hour.

Well, we ate lunch, but we didn't accomplish much after that. The storm did more damage to this city than that caused by the previous year's riots. Most electricity was out, many trees were actually uprooted and blown over, tree limbs littered the streets, many streets and parking lots were flooded to the point where traffic was impossible. Water in one office parking lot was as deep as car windows.

The storm departed as quickly has it had arrived. Silence.

> *The winds and the waves shall obey thy will,*
> *Peace, be still!* [34]

We weaved our way through portions of streets that were still open, hoping to conduct more interviews, but finally gave up. In frustration we returned to our respective hometowns, resigned to the fact that one more trip would be necessary.

The storm story made headlines. Our story was not finished.

Earlier that month, another Mother's Day. Next year, we believed, Maurice Carter would travel to Gary, Indiana, with us to visit his mom. Al Hoksbergen, Mary Blackwell, and I were seated in the cramped quarters of a tiny living room. Mrs. Fowler had just opened her gifts and was still oohing and ahhing as she reached down into the huge basketful of goodies that my kids had prepared for her.

The telephone rang and Mary answered it.

She spoke for a while, and then announced, "It's Maurice."

One would have thought we were in an old-fashioned revival! "Hallelujah! Thank you, Jesus!"

We passed the telephone around.

Next year, my brother. Next year you'll be here!

The Michigan Parole Board set June 15 as the date for the public hearing, to be held in a meeting room at the Duane L. Waters Hospital. The prosecutor and the judge had agreed not to stand in the way of the hearing. Ironically, now that Prosecutor Cherry announced that he had reviewed the medical records and would not oppose the hearing, he was being portrayed as a hero.

Maurice wasn't doing well, and I was worried. His voice was weak. His body was failing. To top it off, our favorite patient had to endure one more episode of torture.

Because Maurice often received medicine intravenously, nurses and other practitioners were having more and more difficulty finding veins. It was decided to transport him to the nearby Foote Hospital in Jackson to have a central line put in. He was anesthetized for the procedure.

Maurice told me, in my next visit with him, that he fully expected to have the line surgically implanted in the chest area. I suspect they must have tried, because when he regained consciousness his chest hurt like the devil. In fact, pain in his chest was so great that he thought they might have broken a bone! The line, however, was inserted in his groin area. And that turned out to be a problem.

I noticed that he was gingerly taking steps and wincing as he walked. The man never complained unless you asked what was going on, and it was apparent to me that something serious was indeed going on.

He was experiencing severe pain in his groin, making it difficult for him to walk, sit, lie, or roll over. He was uncomfortable in every position. The new line had been placed in an uncomfortable location to begin with, but now it was terribly sore. The medical staff took another look. The groin implant had become infected.

Back to Foote Hospital where an impatient physician applied only a localized anesthetic and started yanking on the tube to remove it. Maurice said that he had never experienced such excruciating pain in his life. In a most uncharacteristic manner, he informed that doctor in no uncertain terms that he'd never better try that again. He had been put to sleep for the insertion of this foreign object, and he should have been put to sleep for its removal.

I chose to make this visit very brief. A patient with that kind of discomfort could not enjoy a visit while seated on a steel bench!

It was May 28, and Pat Shellenbarger was determined that this would be his last trip to Benton Harbor to gather information for his upcoming exposé. Lateesha had warned us again, saying that some unsavory people in the 'hood weren't pleased with our continued probing into matters dealing with Billy Lee Brown.

We interviewed some former cops, men who had been officers at the time of the Schadler shooting. Nothing new. We tried to find a woman who claimed to another party that she had been in the store at the time of the shooting. No luck. Then we went out looking for Matty again. I advised Pat to go to the party store where Dawg had picked him up on that eventful night. Bullseye! I spotted him.

The parking lot of this party store was no place for Pat and me to be operating, even in the middle of the day. Pat jumped out of the van. I remained in the front seat. "Hey, Matty."

"Yeah?"

His quick response proved that we had the right guy. I hadn't seen him in a long time and hardly recognized him.

Then someone else hollered to Pat. Talk about bad luck. It was another uncle, the one who Lateesha had secretly recorded. Pat had interviewed him earlier, with no success. Now he was identifying Pat just when he wanted to remain low profile. We quickly got rid of him after making some small talk, then went after Matty again.

"Remember when you met this guy at Dawg's house?" Pat was making the introduction.

Wally looked at me, obviously recognizing me but not remembering when we had met or what we had talked about. He had some teeth in his mouth this time, so he was easier to understand.

"What we talk about?'

"You were telling me about that day when Billy Lee shot that cop, Schadler."

You would have thought Matty had spotted a ghost. He ran to an old Cadillac parked nearby, plunked himself into the passenger's seat, and slammed the door. That inebriated old man moved like he had just been fired from a cannon!

"We're not trying to get you into any trouble," Pat assured him after he persuaded him to roll down the window. I just want you to tell me what you remember."

Matty was mute.

Moments later a woman exited the party store, walked up to the driver's side of the Caddy, and greeted her new passenger. "Hi Matty!"

She must have sensed that he didn't want to talk with us. The car sped off. Wally was gone, and so was another opportunity to shore up the premise of our story.

Virtually all newspapers, even the *Herald-Palladium* in Benton Harbor and St. Joseph, were now calling on the governor to pardon Maurice Carter. The only way he could receive proper treatment was outside the prison walls. It was time.

Disturbing news from Lateesha: People who claim to be from the Schadler family were offering her money if she'd tell them what Pat and I were up to. That's bad news for two reasons. Number one: She's broke, and five hundred dollars sounds pretty good when Pat and I are paying nothing, when one doesn't have a job, and when one has a stack of bills to pay. Number two: One of Schadler's sons is known to talk pretty tough. He had reacted pretty angrily in the courtroom when Pat tried to interview his mother. Lateesha doesn't need blackmail threats.

EIGHTEEN

JUNE 2004

A public hearing, conducted by the Michigan Parole Board, was coming up in two weeks. It was the only thing on my mind. Sleep was elusive, as things that had to be done and decisions that had to be made before June 14 played games with my mind. I finally rolled out of bed in the middle of the night to prepare a list of priorities. Once a game plan was established in writing, sleep would follow.

I had been discussing the issue of where Maurice might live after his release for some time with our daughter Sue, who was managing a large nursing home in Holland, about twenty-five miles from our home. Her nursing home had been inspected and approved by the Michigan parole officer stationed in Holland. Scott Morgan had worked with Sue on other cases and approved the transfer. Maurice's family was comfortable with placing him in that facility. He was expected to remain in Michigan because he would be on parole, and that requires a weekly check-in with a Michigan parole officer. Sue's company wouldn't make much money on this one because Maurice was indigent and would therefore be a Medicaid patient. She had a bed available. Solved for the moment.

Then there was the issue of housing Maurice's family. As I have explained, Maurice's mother is elderly and travel is difficult for her. She and other members of the family, especially Maurice's cousin Mary, would want to visit Maurice in Holland. A roundtrip from Gary might be more than Mrs. Fowler could handle in one day. Our dear friends Dee and Jerry Horne came to the rescue. They own two condominium units on Lake Macatawa in Holland, residing in the upstairs quarters, and keeping the downstairs unit open for special guests. They offered to make the floor-level home available to members of the Carter family when they traveled to Holland. These comfortable accommodations would be perfect. Solved for the moment.

Another issue was transportation for Maurice from Jackson to Holland. Members of the citizens committee wanted to hire a limo to pick up our hero at the prison hospital. On the surface, a good idea. Below the surface, a bad idea. We weren't taking into consideration the health issues. For one thing, his condition could worsen during the 135-mile ride. Besides that, it was important to realize that, because of the medication he takes to maintain his stability, close proximity to a restroom would be imperative. It would be not only uncomfortable but also embarrassing if the limo had to make repeated stops. The simpler answer, a luxurious motor home. The people with the solution: again, Dee and Jerry Horne. They owned a beautiful new coach, and readily agreed to make it available.

We had to prepare testimony on Maurice's behalf for the hearing. All Maurice Carter supporters, especially the legal team and the citizens committee, were most helpful in this effort. We met to discuss specific subjects that each person would cover in his or her brief statement to the board. I had been given strict instructions by Chairman Rubitschun as to the length of statements, and what should and should not be included in them. He preferred that our list of participants be kept relatively short and suggested, as an alternative, that many people who wanted to say something could do so by letter. The letters would be entered into the record and recognized by the board. We agreed that, in my short statement, I would include meaningful quotes from some of those letters, and I would hand over the packet of letters to the parole board. I notified Rubitschun of our plans and was then directed to inform the prison inspector as to the number of people we expected.

It was also important to notify the media. The parole board is not enamored with the media, although I must say that the Michigan Department of Corrections has a good media relations office and officer. I was informed that media representatives were welcome, but that cameras and microphones were forbidden. I faxed this information to the two dozen members of the media who most closely followed our case. I also urged them to notify me if they planned to attend. This would affect the total count, and I wanted to be as accurate as possible. The media people demonstrated a real spirit of cooperation. I made up press kits for the media, checked to determine if courtroom artists would be allowed in place of photographers (the answer was yes), and I listened to the grumbling and the complaints about cameras and microphones. I'm not even sure the position of the parole board is legal, but I was not getting into any arguments at this late date.

Then came a threat to Maurice Carter's safety. Brian Schadler, son of the late Tom Schadler, had been causing trouble behind the scenes. He continually badgered Lateesha about the ongoing investigation that might lead to identification of a different shooter. I don't know how he got her name. He was determined to halt that activity because he was convinced that Maurice Carter was the shooter. "My dad was a good cop," he was quoted as saying, "and he could not have made a mistake on identifying the man who fired the gun at him." Not only did he continue to harass Lateesha, but she claims that he also tried to bribe her, and periodically threatened her. He finally was heard to say that if Maurice Carter ever attained freedom, he was going to do to him what Carter had done to his dad. I interpreted that as a threat on Maurice Carter's life, and as a spokesman for and friend of Maurice I wasn't about to let that slide.

I have contacts in the Michigan State Police, and I arranged a meeting with two high-ranking officers at Fifth District Headquarters in Paw Paw the day before the hearing. I was reassured when these guys didn't think my concerns were frivolous. One of the officers knew the family and new a bit about Brian.

It was arranged to have a Michigan State Police detective in plain clothes pay a call on young Mr. Schadler before the day was over, not only notifying him that the police were aware of his threats, but warning him that he would do well not to cause any problems at the public hearing the next day. I was later told that this visit nearly caused him to blow a gasket.

This was monumental. At last came the day of a public hearing that would help decide whether Maurice Carter would be a free man.

Many of us gathered at the Holiday Inn in Jackson, Michigan, the night before. We ordered out for pizza and pulled tables together in the giant indoor courtyard so that we could work on our statements together. We had family there, we had citizens committee members, and we had part of the legal team. We exchanged ideas and made notes. We wanted to eliminate overlapping if possible, and we wanted to maximize on all the positive things we could think of. We agreed on the order of presentation. Our statements were finalized and timed to fit the Rubitschun requirements. We were ready!

The Public Hearing

By 5:10 a.m. there was no more sleep in me. Scott Elliott topped me. He was already in the hotel coffee shop when I arrived before six.

I drove to the hospital ahead of everyone so that I could greet the media. I knew that reporters would be jockeying for position. By getting there early I had a brief opportunity to see Maurice as he was being led through the lobby to the meeting room. Marcia met him in person for the first time right there and gave him a hug before he was brusquely tugged away by an impatient guard. He was handcuffed and shackled. Did they really believe this dying man was going to run when he was this close to freedom?

There was a brief tug-of-war when a guard insisted that a courtroom artist could not enter the hearing with his materials. The MDOC's PR man had originally approved the request, and he quickly solved this problem.

We were shoehorned into a long, narrow meeting room of the Duane L. Waters Hospital that had not been designed for a gathering like this.

John Rubitschun presided, and while in the spotlight he reviewed the rules one more time and then let it be known again that he believed Mr. Carter was guilty.

Sensing that we all were on this roller coaster ride together, we gripped the sides of our chairs. And, of all things, the trolley nosed downward! A representative from the Michigan Attorney General's office was directed to start the hearing with his series of questions. The man's name was Charles Schettler, and his goal was to state strong opposition on behalf of the Michigan Attorney General to a medical commutation. (We learned from reliable sources that his secret goal was to make the Governor of Michigan, a member of the opposite political party, look soft on crime by granting this commutation!)

He started out with a list of negative-sounding questions to Maurice Carter, his social worker, and a hospital physician, but then took great pains to point out that usually those prisoners seeking a sentence commutation for medical reasons are incapacitated. In fact, he said, the prisoners are often rolled into the hearing on gurneys with tubes running in and out of their bodies. "This man," he exclaimed, "came walking in here under his own power and has full use of his arms and hands." He hadn't listened to a thing the medical people testified about hepatitis C. The AG's office took the position that Maurice could pose a threat to the general public and, therefore, the State of Michigan was opposed to his release.

An astonished Pat Shellenbarger chased Schettler to his car immediately following the hearing, asking him to expand on the State's position that Maurice posed a threat to the public. Said this elected state official: "Our job is to protect the public. He could pick up a gun and blaze away!" His exact words were printed in *The Grand Rapids Press*, bringing immediate disgrace upon Mr. Schettler and his office from within and outside of his own party, and from within and outside of his own state! The general consensus was that Schettler could probably not expect a promotion in the near future after this public display of ignorance regarding hepatitis C and his insensitivity to a dying person.

The roller coaster swooped upward as we presented our well crafted statements. Rubitschun obviously appreciated the manner in which his regulations were observed, calling on me after each statement to announce the name of the next witness. Keith Findley, Rob Warden, Scott Elliott, Lisa Connell, Marcia Tjapkes, Joyce Gouwens, Mary Blackwell, Gary Giguere, Al Hoksbergen, and I all spoke.

Our car peaked and started back down the hill as the chairman called on Sandy Schadler, daughter of the late Tom

Schadler, who was the lone family member to attend. "I think it seems a little bit easy for those who have not been victims to state what is justice," she said. "Mr. Carter has played the role of a victim, and my family has been vilified." She urged Governor Granholm to send a message that would demonstrate support of law enforcement officers by denying commutation of the Carter sentence. "They put their lives on the line every day for us." I didn't recall anyone from our group denying that fact. The statement, it seems to me, didn't conform to the instructions we had been given.

Maurice was granted permission to give the final word, a word that he delivered with a voice weakened by his illness: "I am sixty years old. I am not a threat to anybody. All I want to do is just live the rest of my life in peace." Then he concluded with another masterful stroke of public relations, by thanking the board for giving him the opportunity to speak. "We all know that the system is not perfect and that things do happen," he said. "I happen to be one of those. I just hope one day the truth will come out."

The hearing was over. The board promised a vote by the end of the week.

Reporters swarmed around many of us outside the building, and many of us took a swipe at the Attorney General's representative right away. We would not allow the state's embarrassing gaffe to go unnoticed.

Once again I drove home from Jackson swimming in a sea of emotion. The car radio blared away, but I didn't hear it. I hardly noticed when the cell phone rang.

"Mr. Tjapkes?"

"Yes."

"It's John Rubitschun."

Lord!

"I wanted to call you in private to thank you."

Don't lose control of the car, here!

He thanked me profusely for all the work that I had done on the hearing, having it so well organized, and having everyone carefully observe the 3-minute time constraints. He talked and he talked. Was I dreaming? He finally confided that the board would vote in two days, but he didn't want that information leaked. He also advised me that, after the governor made her decision, based on the board's recommendation, there would be another 28-day wait. My thoughs: *What's twenty-eight days after more than twenty-eight years?*

As we talked my mind darted in different directions. Would he have told me about this 28-day waiting period if he didn't anticipate a positive vote by the board? Did I dare hope?

I prayed.

Late that day, I accepted a call from Maurice. Man, he sounded bad! The ordeal had taken its toll, physically and emotionally. I had to do my job one more time.

I first told him about the call from John Rubitschun. He was speechless. I told him about the media people who were there (which he didn't realize) and about the wonderful sketch artists in the room, whose drawings were already being widely viewed on television. I told him how delighted his supporters were to finally see him in person. I reminded him that we had people drive from as far away as Madison and Chicago just to speak their piece for three minutes.

At the conclusion of the short call, we were talking like old friends again. His voice was stronger. His adrenaline was pumping.

"I love you, Big Bro!"

"Love you, too."

Ready for the June 17 ride?

We head down the slope first.

I received à disturbing e-mail message from Lateesha. A woman who identified herself as Ruth Schadler called her and offered her five hundred dollars to "say things" to the parole board and the governor's office. What in heaven's name did they think she could say?

It was Thursday, the day for the regular Maurice Carter call. I was in our back sunroom at the computer when I clicked on zero to accept the telephone charges.

Just after we began speaking, the computer let out a beep indicating the receipt of an e-mail message.

Being only a few feet away, I casually walked over to the screen as our discussion continued. I interrupted, "Hey Maurice!"

"Yeah."

"Lisa thinks that she just heard a South Bend television station report a yes vote for commutation! She's trying to verify it right now."

"You're kidding me!"

"Get off the phone and call me back in ten minutes."

Lisa and I are good. Turn us loose on a mission and we can cover a lot of territory! I called a news producer at Channel 16 in South Bend. Sure enough, the Associated Press was reporting that the Michigan Parole Board was recommending a medical commutation by a vote of 9-0! I clicked off the phone and wept.

Pulling myself together, I quickly put out a brief note on the Maurice Carter e-mail network.

Then we found the AP story, copied it, and put that out on the network.

Maurice called back. For once I had a chance to give him some good news.

What a thrill to be the one to inform him that he was going to be a free man. I read him the information. For a mo-

ment our excitement got in the way of our words. Then came
the major impact, and we both got pretty weepy.

We couldn't continue. I suggested that he call back on Saturday after we'd both settled down a bit.

Marcia and I ended the day with kids and grandkids, one of
our favorite activities, this time celebrating a Maurice Carter
victory with a pizza party.

"Hey Art, I can't get the phone charger to work."

Race mechanic Art Vaandering and I were headed to Stan-
ton, Michigan, for a weekend that I look forward to all year.
The date was June 25, and it marked the start of the annual
Pure Stock Muscle Car Drags at Mid-Michigan Motorplex.

It was still dark when he wheeled the huge SUV onto a
county back road. Behind the big Ford was an automobile
hauler where my 1963 GT Hawk was proudly perched. This
is a special Hawk, one that Studebaker drivers recognize as
an R-2, meaning that the car is powered by a supercharged
Avanti-V8 engine.

There had been no word from Governor Granholm about
a commutation the day before, and nothing could persuade
me to sit home by the telephone all day Saturday. But now
I had a new problem—my cell phone was not charging, and
that was my only access to the outside world when I was at
the drag strip. We wiggled wires and jiggled contacts, but the
charger refused to function. The only alternative was to turn
off the telephone to save power, and then periodically click it
on to check for messages.

Thanks to Art the car was performing superbly. The time
trials are held on Friday, the first part of the 2-day event. Then
each driver gets paired with another car for a two-out-of-
three shootout on Saturday. I was winning my share of races,
but we couldn't seem to coax any more from the big, heavy

Hawk. We worked on shifting, tuning, even changing the air pressure in the tires. The best I could get in a quarter mile was slightly over fifteen seconds and a speed of slightly better than ninety-one miles per hour. Certainly not bad, but when you're at the drag strip you always want more.

Talk among the Studebaker old timers was that Stude engines seem to enjoy having the timing advanced a bit. Art gave it a try, I made another run, and we did not experience the desired effect. It was the car's worst quarter-mile of the day.

I returned to the pit, asked Art to readjust the timing, and decided that I should check the weakened cell phone for any messages. There were nine. Something had happened.

I discovered that the calls were mostly from the media. As I tried to retrieve messages I repeatedly missed incoming calls. Finally Lisa got through. My phone line had been so busy that she just assumed I had heard the good news: The governor had granted the commutation!

I tried to return as many calls as possible, doing my best to take care of those reporters who had taken such good care of us. The phone battery continued to drain. After forty-five minutes, the telephone was hardly functioning, and I was temporarily caught up.

I looked up, and Art had a strange grin on his face. "The timing has never been set this way before. Give it a try, and I'll do what I can to repair your telephone charger."

I got in the car and prayed out loud this time. "Thank you, Lord! Thank you!" (For the commutation, not for the quick tune-up.)

As I wheeled onto the dragstrip I noticed that I was paired up with Ottawa County's Assistant Prosecutor Doug Mesman. He drives a sweet Pontiac GTO that runs in the mid-14s. I can't beat that car; it's in a different category, but I enjoy racing with an acquaintance. We grinned and waved.

The lights on the Christmas tree blinked down to green and we were off. Holy Cow! Doug wasn't pulling away from me. He was ahead, but he couldn't shake me. Second gear, same thing. Third gear, same thing. This car was cooking! I knew I was going to lose, but I hadn't expected the race to stay so tight. I retrieved my ticket and learned that the Studebaker and I had just made our best time and best speed for a quarter mile: 14.949 seconds, 93.60 miles per hour! I let out a whoop, partly because of Art's incredible intuition in tuning engines, and partly due to elation over what was happening with Maurice.

By late afternoon newsman Brett Thomas from the Grand Rapids NBC Affiliate WOOD TV–8 showed up at the dragstrip with a photographer. Reporters had been asking me for interviews, and I informed them that I would not leave the dragstrip. Brett then chose to come to me. Curious Studebaker drivers wondered what I had going that attracted television cameras to this unlikely location. I did an interview, and then the cameraman insisted on filming the Studebaker as it made a pass down the dragstrip.

Marcia watched the whole report on the six o'clock news. Art and I ended the day with a little sip of Cutty Sark.

I thought he would be excited about the Studebaker's speed and time. Instead, "I'm really jazzed," he said, "about getting this guy out of jail."

So was I!

Saturday was anticlimactic. It was a great weekend. The racing was fun, but the Maurice Carter news was phenomenal.

The route home from Art's mechanic shop takes me past a furniture and rug cleaning business, owned and operated by my friend Mart Bomers. He has one of those little signs in the front yard with changeable letters. He uses it to advertise his services some of the time, but most of the time he uses the sign for editorial comment.

The commutation had made big news in the media all weekend.

A smile crossed my tired face as I drove past Mart's shop. Said the little sign: "THANK DOUG TJAPKES FOR HIS COMPASSION!"

Thank God for his amazing grace.

July 2004

The Coney Island Cyclone is considered by connoisseurs to be the world's most famous roller coaster. I contend that the Maurice Carter Cyclone rivals any roller coaster! Take a simple 31-day period, the month of July, 2004, as an example.

In that period of thirty-one days our car soared up:

Pat Shellenbarger's exposé about the secret tapes pointing to another shooter appeared on the front page of a Sunday edition of *The Grand Rapids Press*.

Our legal team asked Prosecutor Cherry to reopen the investigation with the Innocence Project, based on the tapes.

and plunged down:

Maurice Carter's health nosedived, he nearly died, and he almost gave up.

The public was not permitted to watch Maurice make his final exit from prison.

Skittish care facility operators refused to give this ailing inmate a place to live upon his release.

and then screamed to the highest peak in its history:

FREEDOM!

The bold headlines on the front page of the Sunday *Grand Rapids Press* informed the public that there were secretly recorded conversations in which three friends implicated another man. (At the last minute, the editors decided against printing the name of the new suspect. Pat was not pleased.)

Prosecutor Cherry said that he might reopen the investigation of the Schadler shooting, but he refused to include the Innocence Project in such a venture. The shocking exposé failed to trigger the action we had hoped for.

Then Maurice got *very* sick. It was becoming obvious to all of us that each time he suffered a relapse it seemed worse than the last time, and his recovery seemed to take more time.

I got my first inkling of this problem when he called me at the regular time Thursday evening, July 8. He said he was tired, so he spent the day in bed. (Red flag.) His voice was terribly weak and his speech very deliberate. (Another red flag.) He didn't want to talk any longer than fifteen minutes (just one week earlier we had had an animated conversation that lasted an hour!). (A third red flag.)

Another patient in the prison hospital noticed that Maurice hadn't gotten out of bed for three days. "Hey Carter," he said, "you're just about outta here, man. You can't give up now!"

The unnamed prisoner has no idea what a contribution he made. Even though he was feeling dizzy, Maurice got up, took a shower, and decided that his friend was right. He still sounded tired Saturday, but his spirits were up and his voice was stronger. Thank God!

Preparation for the Big Day

The date for Maurice's release was set: Saturday, July 24, 2004. For the past several years, much of the campaign to free Maurice Carter could be handled by the citizens committee. Leo LaLonde, cooperative public relations officer for the Michigan Department of Corrections, was not about to deal with a whole committee now that we were in the final stages. He called me to set up a meeting. It wasn't an invitation. I was instructed to meet him in the Duane L. Waters Hospital parking lot on Thursday, July 15.

When I drove up he ordered me into his car, and we started driving. Where were we going?

Bombshell number one:
The prison warden would not permit cameras or microphones in the hospital parking lot.

Bombshell number two:
The prison warden wouldn't even allow reporters on the prison/hospital grounds.

Bombshell number three:
The prison warden wouldn't even allow Maurice's friends and supporters on the property!

This was a disappointment after all the fantasizing that we had done about that great day when we would actually see our hero step through the prison doors, never to return.

I started to complain and LaLonde stopped me: "At least he's getting out. Just take what you get."

OK.

The hospital building is located behind a giant prison facility. A long driveway off Cooper Street in the city of Jackson circles around the prison facilities to the hospital parking lot. The hospital and the parking lot are hidden from passing traffic.

Leo stopped at the driveway entrance off Cooper Street, pointed to a graveled area on the north side, surrounded by discarded prison equipment and junk. That's where the media and Carter supporters could wait, he said. He agreed that the motor home carrying Maurice could pause there briefly on its way out so that he could wave to his friends and the reporters. Then the bus would have to move on.

The committee and I had hoped that Maurice could hold a news conference right at the prison, but state officials were having no part of that. Perhaps right nearby, then? Everything in the immediate neighborhood is state property, so that was off limits.

Leo continued to drive around the neighborhood, suggesting various locations. I vetoed all of them, explaining the magnitude of this case and the number of people coming. He was startled by my numbers. Somehow he had expected only a handful.

So, we made a larger circle, and about a mile away discovered a huge parking lot at a shopping center on Parnall Street. That would work. Maurice was scheduled to be released quite early in the morning. These stores wouldn't even be open for business yet. The parking lot would be vacant.

Having reached agreement on a location and having outlined the exit procedures, Leo drove me back to my car. To this point he had been all business. He obviously had other places to go and other things to do. As I opened the car door he uncharacteristically gripped my hand, wished me good luck, and wished Maurice good luck. He nodded toward the hospital. "Not many guys in there have a friend like you."

The black Dodge Intrepid sped away.

Now came the task of informing everyone. I gave explicit instructions to all representatives of the media while committee members made certain that all supporters understood the rules.

"Dad, we've got a problem."

The nursing home in Holland had appeared to be an ideal spot not only for Maurice to reside while he waited for a liver transplant, but also for a public reception upon his release. The facility had a large courtyard, filled with the scent of blooming flowers and the bubbling sounds of a small fountain.

On July 19 we learned that Sue's boss rejected the admission of Maurice. The reasons given involved census, number of Medicaid patients, and on and on. No mention was made that he suffered from hepatitis C, or that he was black, or that he was an ex-convict.

Our daughter has been in this business for years and knows a lot of people. She also knew and loved Maurice and dreaded breaking the news to me. She promptly offered her assistance in finding another place, probably nearer to our home in Spring Lake Township, and started contacting friends and acquaintances. Because of spoken and unspoken issues, the task became complicated.

Nursing home #1—in Grand Haven—no.

Nursing home #2—in Grand Haven—no.

Assisted living center #1—in Grand Haven—no.

Please don't let me have to inform Maurice that nobody will take him! That will hurt more than the pain from the disease!

Success! An assisted living center in Grand Haven agreed to accept Maurice. I liked the fact that it wasn't a nursing home, because I thought that he didn't really need care at that level. This was a nice assisted living facility, and it was nearby.

Thank you!

But, unlike the nursing home in Holland, the assisted living center had no space big enough for Maurice's welcome reception.

The public reception for Maurice, again thanks to dear friends, was quickly moved to a neighborhood clubhouse not far from our house. A perfect location. A spacious facility in a beautiful neighborhood, it would easily handle all of the guests that we anticipated.

The Night Before

Media representatives, supporters, members of the Carter family, and members of our family once again gathered at the Holiday Inn in Jackson on Saturday, July 24. From Toronto came Rubin "Hurricane" Carter, accompanied by Win Wahrer, the Executive Secretary of the Association in Defence of the Wrongly Convicted.

Dee and Jerry Horne were already there. Jerry was in the parking lot washing the enormous windshield of the lavish motor home. Maurice would not only ride in style, he would also have a perfect view of the countryside.

Before the day was over I put Dee and Jerry in my car to show them the way to Duane Waters. The hospital was nearby, but the route in between the two locations was filled with twists and turns.

I set my alarm for 5:30 the next morning.

Free at Last

The alarm worked just fine, but I couldn't find the "off" switch. I did find coffee nearby, and wolfed down a protein bar.

Then I was off for my *last* trip to the Duane L. Waters Hospital. And, for once, the weather was perfect. Even the weather was finally demonstrating a spirit of cooperation on this red-letter day.

My car was the first to arrive at the prison property. It was 6:30.

Within minutes, supporters and media people and equipment started arriving.

I wondered about guards but didn't have to wonder for long. Soon state prison vehicles were prowling around, driven by scowling occupants looking our way. Guards nervously lit cigarettes and swaggered back and forth, keeping a wary eye on our little crowd. Some were even wearing flak vests. I have no idea what the state expected, but it looked like Al Capone was about to be released.

I found a man who appeared to be in charge, introduced myself, and explained what Leo LaLonde had earlier arranged. The motor home would arrive carrying Mr. and Mrs. Horne, my wife Marcia, and Maurice's cousin Mary Blackwell. When the vehicle approached the gravel area, I was to board and we would then proceed to the hospital entrance.

Nope. No way! The guard insisted that only I could enter. I would have to drive the motor home. Now I'm going to tell you something: That vehicle is forty-five feet long! My response was as firm as his. I absolutely refused to drive it.

He conferred with his supervisor, and soon we had everything set just as Leo had arranged it.

At eight o'clock the bus arrived. The guard leaned in, checked the names of everyone aboard, ordered me to get in, and then demanded that we follow his vehicle. I'm surprised he didn't turn on the red lights and siren. We were escorted by prison vehicles front and rear, making sure that Jerry wouldn't misbehave in that fancy home on wheels.

Mary had brought the clothing that Maurice was to wear when he stepped into freedom. As we approached the hospital entrance a guard poked his head in the doorway and demanded the clothes, explaining that he had been assigned the task of delivering the apparel to Maurice. This is a minor issue at this major moment, but I want you to know that choosing the right clothes for this occasion was no small matter. Maurice had been working on it for many weeks. While he was easygoing on a lot of issues, he gave very specific instructions to Mary and me ... right down to the kind of cap and the brand of shoes. I knew some of the clothing wouldn't fit well. Maurice insisted on giving everyone his old measurements, refusing to take into consideration that this critical illness had resulted in severe weight loss. It was not worth arguing about.

Mary and I were ordered to step out. The rest were instructed to stay put.

The moment was near.

We made small talk in the waiting room. I was thinking about a statement I had given the press earlier, when asked about my thoughts on Maurice's being set free. I had said, "I'll believe it when I see it."

A usually stern-faced lady at the desk seemed to have caught the spirit of the moment. "Don't just sit there like you're glued to those chairs. Come on over here and watch him come down the steps," she ordered goodnaturedly. We quickly complied.

We heard movement in the clearance area. I was breathing faster than normal. Maurice was coming out, without handcuffs and shackles, his final exit. The scene is indelibly burned into my memory bank. Flanked by guards, he gingerly made his way down the steps. He spotted Mary and me in the lobby, and that grin spread from ear to ear.

Mary received the first hug. Then he threw his arms around me. A reporter later asked me what my first words were, and I quickly answered that there weren't any. Maurice wept. I wept. Finally he said, "I love you." I responded in kind. We were unable to say anything else. We walked through those front doors and down the sidewalk, Mary on one side, me on the other … both of us carrying his few belongings so that he could walk and hold up his pants at the same time.

"Quick, snap it!" Marcia was urging Dee Horne. Click. This was and is the only picture of Maurice leaving the prison because, as you may recall, photographers weren't allowed in the parking lot. It was shot through the window of the motor home.

Jerry Horne is a big man, and he gave Maurice a big hug as he helped the former inmate into the motor home. It was their first meeting. Then everyone wanted hugs. We were interrupted by the burly guard who wanted us out of there. Jerry was given instructions, once again, to follow the escort vehicle. In lieu of any sirens by the state vehicles, he gave the melodic air horns a brief burp.

I advised Jerry that we would have to pause for a moment by the gravel area, where nearly 100 supporters and reporters were waiting, many carrying signs and placards. I turned over my car keys to our daughter Cindy. I wanted to ride to Spring Lake with my brother.

Jerry made the brief stop, opened the door so that I could hand keys to Cindy, and the crowd burst into applause. Photographers, capturing the moment, snapped Maurice's picture through the windows as he smiled and waved. Another beautiful moment, one of many that we would experience on this glorious day.

I sing because I'm happy, I sing because I'm free! [6]

Maurice took the seat of honor, a large recliner in the front of the bus, and relaxed with his feet propped up.

The giant coach gently rounded the sharp turn into the shopping center parking lot. As the door opened, the crowd once again burst into applause. We helped Maurice down the steps, allowing him as much time as he needed, first to greet his family members and my family members, then to give statements to the media. He answered questions and chatted with friends. Maurice was at his best!

Before we returned to our seats, those dear people Terry and Chuck Kelly, who arguably had stuck with Maurice longer than any other friends, presented him with his own cellular telephone. They gave him quick instructions on how to operate it and informed him that the telephone service would be added to their bill.

The guest of honor was again placed in the seat of honor, his feet propped up. Dee and Jerry, having stocked the larder with Maurice's favorite snacks and drinks, made sure he was comfortable. We waited on him hand and foot. As Jerry steered our chariot onto the expressway, I could not imagine

Maurice's thoughts and feelings. Diet Pepsi, potato chips, an expansive panoramic view of the sun-drenched countryside through picture window; a chair more comfortable than any he had ever occupied in the past twenty-nine years; some of his dearest friends surrounding him, along with conversations with one friend after another thanks to the miracle of wireless telephones. Behind bars one minute. In a seat of ultimate luxury the next. There was no one more deserving.

Jerry Horne shared later that one of the most thrilling moments of his life was that 3-hour drive from Jackson to Spring Lake, Michigan. Maurice was on the telephone almost the entire period. "Not once did he say an unkind word," said an astonished Jerry. He didn't badmouth the prison system, the judicial system, the people who treated him so shabbily, but instead gave all of the glory and praise to God.

> *Lord, make me an instrument of thy peace:*
> *Where there is hatred, let me sow love;*
> *Where there is injury, pardon...* [35]

We arrived at the Wildwood Springs Lodge located near our home and our church at noon. Thanks to the wonderful citizens committee and my wonderful family, hamburgers and cheeseburgers were being cooked for everyone on a giant outdoor grill.

Our daughter Sue, her husband Jon, and their twin 3-year-old sons Brenden and Zachary had remained in Spring Lake to coordinate the reception, forgoing the visit to Jackson. The twins, who had been impatiently waiting for this moment, were among the first to greet Maurice as he stepped out of the motor home. We have delightful pictures of that first encounter, one of which made the front page of the local newspaper.

Maurice was definitely the man of the hour. People from

our extended families, our church family, the citizens committee, the legal team, and even our community came out to
welcome him and hug him. He loved the taste of non-prison
food, but I don't know how he ever found time to eat any of
it. And there were two momentous experiences still awaiting
him.

A minivan approached the front of the lodge; the driver
got out, came around the front of the vehicle and opened
the passenger door. Out stepped Mrs. Fowler. I raced up to
greet her and received a warm embrace. Then, Mary and I
each took an arm of this frail, little woman and approached
the building. Someone alerted Maurice that a special guest
had arrived, and walked him to the entrance. Mother and son
looked at each other. Silence for a moment. I cannot describe
the sound that emitted from that dear woman's mouth next,
except to say that it was loud. In my mind, it represented a
mixture of emotions including ecstasy, agony, glory, pain, and
excitement. Michael McArdle, photographer for the *Gary Post-*

Mother and son reunite

Tribune, continuously snapped the shutter on his digital camera and caught a series of amazing pictures, one of which appeared on the front page of his newspaper. Flashbulbs were popping from all directions. People were openly weeping. Maurice was reunited with his mother as a free man. They em-

braced, kissed, and, consistent with her lifestyle, prayed.

I said there were two momentous experiences. The second was about to occur.

Maurice was back at his table, once again trying to savor the flavor of the outdoor barbecue goodies. The crowd had thinned; many had other things to do on this Saturday afternoon. Someone touched Maurice from behind. He turned around and looked directly into the face of Gwen Baird.

Maurice had never met in person this tower of strength, the store clerk

**Surprise visitor
Gwen Baird**

whose story had remained consistent since the day of the crime: Maurice Carter was *not* the shooter!

More hugs. More tears. More flashbulbs.

The day was nearing an end, and we had a lot of cleaning up to do in the lodge.

Maurice was scheduled to move into his new home on Monday. Our oldest daughter and her husband, Cindy and Lee Ingersoll, along with their two children, Betsi and Max, would play host for the rest of the weekend. He loved the Ingersoll family. ("That's part of *my* family!" he announced.) Their home was ideal, designed with a guest bedroom on the main floor with its own private bath. We couldn't wait for him to see it.

It was fun making the casual drive with Maurice through our neighborhood for the first time, pointing out the Hamm family home, our home, Pastor Al Hoksbergen's home, and then arriving at the Ingersoll residence. We all live in the same subdivision. He had been hearing about all of this for years, but now he was actually there.

The guest room was gaily decorated; Betsi and Max had placed a welcome sign on the queen-sized bed. It was large, it was soft. No more steel bunks that often gave him backaches. Here's where he would spend his first night as a free man, and he loved it.

He took one long, hot shower. Pretty soon he took another! "It takes two showers to get rid of that prison funk!" he exclaimed.

Maurice Carter was no longer inmate number #145-902. His calls and his letters would no longer be monitored by the Department of Corrections. He could talk when he felt like it, eat when he felt like it, travel when he felt like it.

The overnight transition from one lifestyle to another could not have been easy. Accustomed to living alone, he often shut the door to the bedroom and spent much of his first couple of days in privacy, and much of that time on the telephone. Cindy and Lee heard him talking with friends on the west coast into the middle of the night.

That special day in history, July 24, 2004, came to an end.

My daily log, called "Countdown to Freedom," began on June 1, 2001, and ended three long years later.

My final entry:

> **"I poured a drink.**
> **"The countdown to freedom had ended."**

> *Free at last! Free at last!*
> *Thank God Almighty, we're free at last!* [36]

It was a beautiful Sunday morning, and Cindy had decided against going to church. Instead, she prepared a nice breakfast for Maurice, his first in this delightful, free atmosphere. After breakfast the two of them sat on the outside deck. It's a deck on the back of the house, facing a beautiful forest of trees in mature Lake Michigan dunes. He was basking in freedom and sunshine and love, and raving about sleeping in that big bed. "It was just like sleeping on a cloud," he said.

Saturday had been a long day, even for those of us who were healthy. We gave Maurice plenty of space on Sunday. He needed to just hang out.

By evening, however, we had plans. I had been enjoying Maurice for years, but now everyone in our family wanted to catch up, and right now! We planned a meal so that he could sample some of Jon Hamm's outdoor cooking skills. The grill was fired up, and Jon lived up to his reputation, preparing a delicious, delectable combination of Angus beef steaks and freshly caught Lake Michigan salmon that had Maurice talking for the rest of his life. Doctors warned us that in his condition Maurice might not have much of an appetite. They were wrong. Right to the very end, they were wrong.

> *Discrimination is a hellhound that gnaws at Negroes*
> *in every waking moment of their lives to remind them that the*
> *lie of their inferiority is accepted as truth in the*
> *society dominating them.* [37]

"Is Mr. Tjapkes there?"

On Monday morning, July 26, I was at the home of Cindy and Lee, ready for a busy day with Maurice. Our plans for the day included moving him to the assisted living facility, checking in with his parole officer, and getting those terrible prison-issue eyeglasses replaced with something chic, in that order.

Who could have tracked me down that early in the day?

The woman on the other end of the line was obviously agitated. She was a corporate executive with the company that operated the home where we were planning to move Maurice. Somehow, she was angry with *me*. She wasn't about to accept Maurice Carter as a resident of her facility. While she didn't go into detail about his race or his status with the Department of Corrections, she made it clear that such an admission would never be permitted without, among other things, polling the other residents.

There was no point arguing with her. I was already embarrassed that this discussion was taking place right in front of Maurice.

The previous week we had been rejected by three nursing homes and an assisted living facility in our community. Today, another turned us away. Of course, the reasons given were legitimate and legal, having been filtered through corporate attorneys in order to survive any challenges.

All family members started over again in the quest for living quarters. It was wonderful that Maurice could reside at

Cindy and Lee's house for the weekend, but he needed more care than they could provide. The man had a disease with a death sentence, complicated by diabetes. This required daily medication, daily monitoring, and diet control. We pulled strings, we made telephone calls to friends, we worked. We had a man here without a home.

... there was no room for them in the inn.
—Luke 2:7

As we encountered refusal after refusal, I cannot describe the rising feelings of disgust and discouragement, like bile coming up in my throat. The rest of the family continued calling. Maurice and I had errands that could not be postponed.

Chrystal Schulist, who had been assigned as Maurice's parole officer worked in the Holland office. That made sense, because that's where we thought Maurice was going to be living. Even though we have a parole officer located in our community, the Holland assignment stuck. We didn't mind. Maurice enjoyed the ride.

We gained immediate access to the parole officer, who was quite businesslike for our first meeting. She did all of the talking at first. Provisions of his parole included not consuming any alcoholic beverages (something he couldn't do anyway with a liver that was, according to one doctor, 90 percent shot), he was permitted to go to restaurants that served alcohol but not joints that primarily served alcohol but also served food, he was expected to report to his parole officer weekly, and he was not permitted to leave the state.

Maurice explained that his family and his elderly mother lived in Indiana, and that he would like to visit them. There was a firm no. Never? *Never!*

As was his custom, Maurice concluded the meeting by thanking Schulist for her time and for her clear and concise explanation of the parole conditions. He was rewarded not only with a slight smile, but with a relationship that improved over time.

I spotted a Burger King across the street. "It's time for you to sample your first Whopper!"

As I had to learn time and again, Maurice wasn't familiar with the routine … a simple routine of waiting in line, placing your order, paying your bill, picking up your order, and choosing your table. He would wander back to the counter, pick up a part of his order, walk back to ask another question. My almost impatient response was quickly repressed by the sober thought that this man hadn't been in society for nearly thirty years. As Rubin Carter explained to me, "He hasn't even opened a door by himself for thirty years! Someone always did it for him." Of course he didn't know the routine.

What he did know was that the taste of a Whopper exceeded that of any hamburger that he had consumed behind bars. He prepared his table as if he were about to enjoy a feast, deliberately setting the fries in one spot, then salting them; unwrapping the hamburger and placing it in the proper location; inserting the straw in his giant tub of diet cola. He audibly savored each bite. I enjoyed watching him eat so much that I was ignoring my own food. The food was delicious for Maurice. The sight was delicious for me.

The experience in the fast food joint was the first of many that Marcia and I found ourselves facing. We were overly sensitive, as the realization hit us, that Maurice had beautiful social skills, but his field was limited. The cellular telephone, for example, still hadn't been invented when he was locked up. He didn't mean to be rude when he answered his cell phone while visiting with friends, and then kept them waiting as he chatted endlessly. In some ways, it was like we had just adopted a young child. We attempted to sensitively and lovingly make corrections and adjustments in a manner that would prevent, at all costs, hurt feelings.

I took the scenic route home from Holland, traveling along the shore of Lake Michigan. It was the first time he had seen the big lake in almost thirty years.

"Are you the Maurice Carter whose picture is on the front page of today's newspaper?"

We hadn't expected to encounter that level of effervescence in a small eyeglass shop in downtown Spring Lake. The question was asked by owner/manager Cindy Westra, personable optometrist whose billboards promise new eyeglasses in an hour. Maurice was proud to respond in the affirmative. In fact, we had a stash of the day's newspapers in the back seat of our car.

"Hey, Big Bro, go get one of those newspapers, would you?" (In Maurice's dialect, "Bro" was pronounced "Bruh." How I wish I could hear it once more.)

I ran to the car and returned with the publication displaying a picture of Maurice on the front page in living color.

"Before you leave, I want you to autograph that newspaper for me," said Cindy, who immediately made this her personal project. "But first, let's find something to make you look better!"

She led him to the display of frames, frowning at some, smiling at some, and finally stating: "This is it! This is you!"

She was right.

She led Maurice into a small room where a doctor could conduct a complete examination. I could see dollar figures accumulating on our bill for this visit.

Marice had not a hint of glaucoma, which was great news. The specifications for the new glasses were transferred to the technicians, and they began working on his new set of specs. Within an hour, everything was finished, just as promised in the ad.

Cindy did some modifications and made some adjustments, chirping all the while about how handsome he looked wearing the new frames. The old pair went into the garbage ... another prison memory permanently discarded.

Then she announced that everything today was on the house. "Congratulations, Maurice Carter! It was a pleasure meeting you."

He looked like a new man.

One less bill to pay. I *felt* like a new man.

Even though he had no place to lay his head, Maurice was riding high when we reentered the car. A message waited on my cell phone.

I quickly dialed my home number and learned that Marcia had good news. After a frustrating day of negative responses, she found success. Our new hero was a quiet, Christian man named Richard Barding who operated a small assisted living facility out in the middle of nowhere. Marcia insisted that Maurice and I go see him right away.

We crossed the bridge onto US 31 south. I followed Marcia's directions and in no time I was driving on back roads in Ottawa County that I had never seen before. The blacktop came to an end, and we continued on a gravel road. The road sign said DEAD END, but we still went on ahead. I think Maurice was having second thoughts, now. So was I.

Just before the end of the road we spotted a small sign and an almost unnoticeable driveway. Following Marcia's directions, we drove to the very end where we found a pleasant looking home nestled in the woods.

We were welcomed by Mr. and Mrs. Barding and given a quick tour of the facility. It appeared to be very comfortable.

Then we sat down to discuss the situation with them. They were completely aware of Maurice's identity, his story, and his health condition, yet they were willing to accept him. God bless the Bardings.

The census was very low, which meant that Maurice could have a room to himself, something that none of the other facilities could promise.

From his bed Maurice could look out a nearby window and see all kinds of wildlife. We were deep in the woods. There was no doubt in my mind that he would see deer, rabbits, wild turkeys, squirrels and who knows what else. If he remained healthy enough, he would view the Michigan seasons change in a most delightful way.

Maurice was so enthused that he wanted to move right away.

Our kids have vans that can hold a lot of belongings, so they joined in the operation. Maurice was moved into a new home, with an atmosphere so casual and informal that he was even allowed access to the kitchen if he seemed hungry. A nurse visited the home on a regular basis, but there were no medical people on staff. That didn't seem important right now. It was up to Maurice to take his medicine and watch his diet.

Marcia and I brewed a pot of flavored decaf coffee and crashed. The pace of this busy day had left us steam-less.

It's important that I bring up this subject.

If I receive any credit for being Maurice Carter's advocate for the previous seven years, my significant other gets the credit for being his advocate during his final three months.

In his consistently amazing planning, God had placed this woman close to Maurice when he needed her the most. Marcia has a background of some twenty years as a registered hospice nurse, with a specialty in pain management. After that she obtained her certification as a parish nurse. Who better to oversee his medical care upon his release?

Her work, her advice, her guidance, her directions, and, yes, her scolding and chiding, had a direct bearing on the length of time Maurice was able to live in freedom. Without Marcia and her watchful eyes 24/7 for three months, we would have lost him sooner. It's as simple as that. She not only had to stay on his case about what to eat and drink, what not to consume, and how to regulate his medicine, she also had to constantly consult with Maurice's caregivers. She had to discuss matters with physicians. She had to update family members. And she had to regulate those of us who were around him every day so that we didn't allow him to violate rules. The occasional winking and violating a rule, or looking the other way in order to make an exception to a rule, wasn't a joke to her. It was a life and death matter.

Maurice sometimes kidded Marcia about her enforcement of the rules, but he genuinely respected not only her knowledge but her concern and love for him.

The official title for the infection is methicillin-resistant staphylococcus aureus. The acronym is MRSA, pronunced "Mersa." Very simply put, it's an infection that is immune to most antibiotics. Doctors hate it. Hospital officials dread it and enforce strict isolation rules if a case is located in their institution. MRSA has long been a problem in prisons, the military, hospitals, and nursing homes, especially where patients with weakened immune systems are more vulnerable to infection.

According to some publications, MRSA has become a problem because, over the years, there has been so much use of antibiotics to kill infections. Now some strains of staphylococcus have become resistant to many drugs that have, in the past, routinely killed the bacteria.

Doctors tell us that the staph infection usually starts as a skin irritation that looks something like a boil, but it can grow, becoming painful and sometimes itchy. The U.S. Center for Disease Control and Prevention has said that there are still a few drugs capable of treating MRSA. But the agency adds that such infections can also be life-threatening.

Jail inmates are among those listed as having the greatest risk of developing an MRSA infection.

Maurice was settling in to his new home in the woods and was enjoying it. On Tuesday our son-in-law Lee took him to visit the parole officer and then enjoyed the afternoon with him, eating hamburgers and driving from here to there. How Maurice enjoyed riding in the front seat of that van with Lee. The feelings went both ways, actually. Lee always jumped at the opportunity to provide transportation for Maurice.

On Wednesday morning I stopped in to see him, and he wasn't making any sense. A visitor from our church was there, hoping to take him to lunch. Maurice wasn't dressed and wasn't having much success getting dressed.

I quickly asked a staff member what was going on. They were not versed on his disease symptoms and thought he was just a bit out of sorts. I knew better.

I sent his visitor home and rushed home to confer with Marcia. It didn't sound good to her, but for a second opinion I called Scott Morgan at the prison. I described what was going on. "ER right now," said Scott. "He's heading toward a coma!"

I drove back out those country roads at breakneck speed. Marcia called ahead and asked that the staff get him dressed. He walked so slowly, just as he talked, but I eventually got him into the car. As ill as he was, he recognized that we were not wasting time. The pedal was to the metal.

Marcia called ahead. They were waiting for us at the Emergency Room of North Ottawa Community Hospital in Grand Haven.

Doctors and nurses took over, and it wasn't looking good. Marcia remained at his side as I ran some errands.

Maurice was hardly conscious and was not rational. In addition, we noticed that his body was covered with sores, some of them bleeding.

As the doctors gave him a thorough exam they asked about the sore in his groin, saying that it was badly infected. Well, that answers a few questions about his method of walking.

Our own physician got involved.

Late in the day, tests showed that he was quickly responding to treatment to lower the ammonia level. And then the dreaded word MRSA. Thanks to the Michigan Department of Corrections, Maurice H. Carter was not only battling hepatitis C, he was fighting a serious staph infection, the worst of its kind. While documents show that this is not uncommon among prisoners, in Maurice's case it was particularly outrageous, because he was incarcerated for something he didn't do. During his time behind bars, he contracted not one but two serious threats to his health.

Our doctors checked with Henry Ford Hospital in Detroit, and hospital officials there would have no part of evaluating a patient for a liver transplant if there was a staph infection out of control. So now the treatment took on a new dimension. We had to fight health problems with a double attack. Maurice would stay here for a while, and he was quarantined.

Those of us who chose to see him had to wear a mask, latex gloves, and a gown. That wouldn't stop us.

He was doing much better the next day when I visited him. It was amazing how fast he would recover when the ammonia level dropped.

On the positive side, he loved the hospital food. He showed me the menu, amazed at the variety of foods he was allowed to order.

And after he ate each delicious meal, he made a telephone call to the kitchen: "This is Maurice Carter in Room 219. I just finished a wonderful meal, and I wanted you to leave word that the chef is to be commended!" The sweet little woman on the other end of the line was speechless.

That was our Maurice.

The emergency dash to the hospital brought to an end his first stay in the assisted living facility. The frightened owner said that he didn't have the staff to handle a problem like that and declined to take him back.

The hospital social worker located a room at another facility at a sensational geographic location. The older style building was nestled on the banks of the Grand River in a little community called Lamont, about halfway between Grand Haven and Grand Rapids. Our daughter Sue's first full-time nursing home position had been at this facility. The view was spectacular.

And, in typical Maurice Carter fashion, within minutes he had worked his way into the hearts of nearly everyone on the staff. He's probably the first patient in their history to have staff members driving a few miles to buy him a hamburger and fries. By that time, the Angus Steakburger had taken precedence over the Whopper. He loved a hamburger. And staffers loved the guy. But then, who didn't?

The hospital visit was not his last. Two weeks later, another relapse. A couple weeks after that, another. That time he was taken to Butterworth Spectrum Hospital in Grand Rapids.

During his three months of freedom, there were mad dashes to the hospital about every two weeks when ammonia levels soared. The problem was that his caregivers had to be extremely careful in the regulation of Maurice's diet and medication. Because of frequent lapses in that intensity of care, Marcia would then have to step in. My wife was finally involved on a nearly full-time basis.

In between those relapses, however, we had some absolutely wonderful experiences.

AUGUST 2004

"I've waited ten years to do this." I could get no more words out of my mouth. Someone in the congregation said something out loud. Someone else started clapping. The applause became tumultuous. I motioned to Maurice to join me on the platform in the Ferrysburg Community Church. He wasn't walking all that well, but he made it up the three steps, and we embraced. The hug lasted and the people jumped to their feet.

When things quieted down Maurice took the microphone.

"I came here because I wanted to let you all know that I am truly, truly grateful for your love, your support, and your encouragement during the struggle for my freedom."

And then, in typical Maurice Carter style, he added "Isn't God wonderful?'

Applause.

It was Sunday, August 15, and it had taken a while to get Maurice dressed and ready for a worship service. He referred to our church as his church, and he was so ready for the experience of meeting for the first time this body of diligent supporters. It was a beautiful moment for our family and for Maurice, because this church, our church, had stood at our side in the battle to free Maurice for years.

In October 2000 Carolyn Yost, special writer for *The Banner*, official publication of the Christian Reformed Church, wrote a feature story about our church's involvement in the Maurice Carter case. The headline read, "Church Members Work to Free Prisoner."

In May 2001, *Muskegon Chronicle* staff writer Terry Judd wrote a story about us entitled "Local Church on a Freedom Crusade."

For a while we were holding weekly prayer meetings at the church specifically asking for his freedom. Maurice was often mentioned in the congregational prayer. Clippings were regularly updated on the church bulletin board. Members of the kids' choir prayed for Maurice every week. And, of course, members of my own choir had to pray for Maurice, or I wouldn't let them sing.

In preparing for this worship service, I asked one of my favorite singers, gospel soloist Ben Reynolds of Grand Rapids, if he would join us to perform Maurice's favorite hymn, "His Eye Is on the Sparrow." I cannot describe my personal thrill as I accompanied this outstanding singer on the piano. As God would plan things, a former pastor from California and a dear friend of our family, Keith Tanis, was the guest speaker of the day. Keith had been following my trek with Maurice from the first day, and he did a great job not only with the sermon, but with the entire service.

Maurice had chosen a Psalm for Keith to use as the basis for his sermon (40:1-3):

I waited patiently for the Lord; he turned to me and heard my cry.
He lifted me out of the slimy pit, out of the mud and mire;
he set my feet on a rock and gave me a firm place to stand.
He put a new song in my mouth, a hymn of praise to our God.
Many will see and fear and put their trust in the Lord.

As Keith explained to me, "It had been David's song three millennia ago. But Maurice Carter could have sung it just as well. As the text filtered through me that morning, I shared the timeless truth that 'the way out is always up!' Maurice has embodied that truth. 'You may end up in a pit, but don't let the pit end up in you!' Maurice has shown us how."

Media representatives were welcome to attend, and they mobbed Maurice for interviews after the service. This must have been one of the best-publicized church services in Christian Reformed Church history. And while I do not mean to minimize the impact on Maurice, I must tell you that this service touched everyone.

After he had spoken, Maurice returned to his pew near the front of church. I walked over to the keyboard to begin the musical part of the service. Marcia told me later that, when Maurice sat down, our grandson Max jumped over the back of the next pew, plunked down next to Maurice and snuggled up to him. A more serious-minded woman of the congregation saw Max make his move and shared later that this little incident cleared out any doubts in her mind about Maurice Carter. I tell you, he touched people!

I asked Keith about his memories of that day. He said, "In the church year, Sundays in August are called 'ordinary time.' No special seasonal observances like Christmas, Easter, or Pentecost drive the services during ordinary times.

"The ordinary folks that gathered in church that far-from-ordinary Sunday sang their hearts full. God had used us, after all, to be God's hands and mind and will to lift Maurice out of the pit of prison. God had used my friend and brother Doug, a newsman, to bring Good News to Maurice Carter. We came together that Sunday in ordinary time to celebrate God's salvation of Maurice and each of us. For most Christians around the world, it was 'ordinary' time. But that Sunday, August 15, was no ordinary Sunday in Ferrysburg Community Church. On that Sunday, we left with the joy of Christmas, the hope of Easter, and the strength of Pentecost! It was no ordinary Sunday! And we will never be the same."

His eye is on the sparrow,
And I know he watches me! [6]

On another day in the middle of August, a warm, sunny day along the Grand River in Lamont, Michigan, Maurice Carter entertained three guests. Pat Shellenbarger, our investigative reporter friend at *The Grand Rapids Press,* brought along two of his coworkers. Ed Golder was the gutsy editorial writer who, despite the conservative reputation of his newspaper, campaigned in earnest with several tough pieces on behalf of Maurice. The third man was Charles Honey, religion editor for the *Press.* I wasn't at that meeting, so I'm going to quote freely from a poignant column that was published the following Saturday, August 21, on the religion page of the *Press,* authored by Mr. Honey:

> This week, I had the privilege of meeting a man convicted of trying to kill someone.
> His name is Maurice Carter. He has gentle eyes, a warm hug, and a soft smile that glows with gratitude.
> In this thin, ailing man, I saw a presence of grace that I have not witnessed in a very long time.
> "I know this God is for real," Carter said quietly. "He's just answered my prayers. That's what keeps me going."

Honey's column, entitled "Maurice Carter knows 'It's so great to be free'" then went on to review the Carter case in some detail, as well as the steps that led to his freedom.

But it wasn't the details of his case that drew me to Carter. It was his lack of bitterness after losing the prime of his life to prison. In him, I saw the power of faith to transform and transcend.

Maurice readily admitted to the trio that after his conviction he was frustrated, bitter and angry, and that he "sort of" lost his faith. He gave me more credit than I deserved for his turnaround.

"I know what he put me on this earth for now. He wants me to help others. That's what life is all about—being around good people and doing God's work."

The conclusion of the column brings tears to my eyes.

But until his health improves, Carter is just drinking in the beauty of being alive. He rhapsodized about eating steak and salmon from Doug and Marcia Tjapkes' grill, and about how he felt when he got out of prison.

"It was just a great day," he said, hands open. "I felt the breeze, I saw the sun. It's so great to be free."

We walked out back of the nursing home, where fish jumped in the Grand River and a light breeze blew through the soft sunshine. Standing next to Maurice Carter, I was grateful to be alive—and free.

That's our Maurice! The impact that he made on the life of Mr. Honey is very similar to the way he touched countless lives!

> *God is so good, God is so good,*
> *God is so good, He's so good to me.* [38]

Another special visitor in August was Alex Kotlowitz.

Alex made the long drive from the Chicago area just to spend some quality moments with his dear friend, a man whom he had not yet met in person.

Maurice loved to go out to eat, and Alex had skipped lunch to get there on time. I suggested that we drive to a nearby Arby's.

The two men genuinely loved each other. I saw my job that day mainly as a chauffeur. I helped Maurice in getting the food that he wanted, got the guys set up at a table off in a corner, and pretty much stayed out of the conversation.

Of all the visits, the times most cherished by Maurice were those with members of his family. Mary Blackwell helped to coordinate those precious moments, bringing her sister and other family members, even an old girlfriend. These were not just brief visits. They gobbled up the better part of a day and they did wonders for his morale.

The gang would hop in Mary's car and head to a mall for some clothes shopping, which was one of Maurice's favorite activities. He took pride in dressing well and loved shopping even more than my wife does. Then they would go to a nice restaurant. No fast food joints for this group. It seemed as though he couldn't get enough tasty food to erase the memories of the garbage that had been forced on him in the prison system for nearly thirty years.

SEPTEMBER 2004

The board of directors of INNOCENT! held its first meeting in the building that housed our new quarters—the old, old Muskegon County Jail. Does God have a sense of humor or what?

Jerry Horne had graciously donated this office space to our venture. The owner of the Manpower franchise for this part of Michigan, he had extra space in the Manpower building in Muskegon. The gift of office space plus utilities was such a meaningful contribution toward the continued success of INNOCENT!

It was at this meeting that the board approved hiring me as a full time, salaried manager of the operation. At last I could think about phasing out of the church organ business. Actually, I had been devoting far more than forty hours a week to INNOCENT! already. But now I would get paid for it (if and when there was money).

I gave Maurice the good news the next morning, and he radiated excitement. The first phase of his expansive dream of providing assistance to prisoners was becoming a reality.

That was really his dominant dream. He envisioned national exposure. There was no doubt in his mind that he would have a book published in future years. The two of us would travel together so that he could speak with high school kids, attend book signings, lecture church groups, and so on. We would do our best to change things in the world so that prisoners would not have to undergo experiences similar to his.

On the lighter side of that dream, Maurice pictured us traveling in his Cadillac. That's what he used to drive, and that's what he wanted now. As he and I traveled around western Michigan, he would spot a nice, newer model Cadillac. "Look at that! See, we don't need a brand new Cadillac." He assured me that he would even let me drive it. Some of the time.

Another favorite dream involved his future lifestyle. The trees along the Grand River were just beginning their transformation from summer green to autumn yellows and reds. He and I were leaning against the nursing home fence that prevented patients from falling down the banks and into the river. From there we could watch families and fishermen passing in their boats; fish on the far side of the river were jumping out of the water to feast on bugs, and an occasional small tree limb lazily spun and twisted its way toward Lake Michigan.

"This is where I want to live, man. I'm not going back to Gary, and that kind of life. I'm going to find a little house in the Tri-Cities area, maybe where I can see the river like this. Then I'm going to bring Moms here to live with me. It doesn't have to be big and fancy. Just something nice. I'm going to be with good people doing good things!"

I know it's important to get away. I've heard all the lectures about leaving your troubles behind. As I've explained earlier, drag racing rates near the top of the list of my favorite activities.

September 17 and 18 were the fall dates for the Pure Stock Muscle Car Drags. Mechanic Art Vaandering, nephew Tom Kuiper, and I were there. The Hawk performed well. I drove well. We had a great time.

But back home Maurice's health was failing, and we were getting nowhere fast in our quest to conquer a staph infection so that he could get properly evaluated for a potential liver transplant. The repeated hospital admissions were taking their toll. This was no life for him. Deep down, I feared that we were losing the battle.

When I went to Stanton, the black cloud accompanied me. The weekend was fun, but I didn't race with total abandon. Too much on my mind.

On September 27, Marcia and I celebrated our wedding anniversary by getting away for a few days. It was the perfect opportunity to combine business with pleasure. I wanted to visit several prisoners in Michigan's beautiful Upper Peninsula, and Marcia and I loved to visit and travel in the UP. I booked a room facing the Straits of Mackinac where we could look out over the water and see magnificent Mackinac Island. Others would monitor Maurice for a few days.

A word of explanation here. The reason we had to stay so close to Maurice was because I was the one who was most able to detect any chemical imbalances quickly. I knew Maurice so well that I could spot slowness of speech and/or loss of memory for what they were. Nursing home personnel, so accustomed to the erratic behavior and speech patterns of old folks, would take these symptoms in stride and often ignore them. In Maurice's case, that could be fatal. If he didn't receive prompt treatment, the ammonia level would skyrocket to a height that would send him into a coma.

There was no alternative. I either had to talk to him by telephone or visit him *every* day. We learned the hard way that we just couldn't take any chances.

On those occasions when I spotted or heard something irregular, Marcia would take the next step, contacting those people who had the ability and the authority to restore some sense of normalcy. This Maurice Carter freedom thing took on a life of its own and evolved into a full-time job for both of us.

In later months we took turns second-guessing what could or should have been done, but I respectfully submit that no other husband-and-wife team could have improved on our three-month performance record. We tried hard and we meant well.

TWENTY-TWO

OCTOBER 2004

"Are you giving up with Maurice?"

The blunt question startled me. It came from Linda Dykstra, a member of our church choir, immediately following our rehearsal on Thursday, October 14. Each week, before the singing begins, various choir members share prayer requests. I must have inserted an extra amount of passion in my plea for Maurice Carter prayers this time. His health was failing rapidly.

Linda is a psychologist, and an instant friendship grew between us when she and her husband joined our church. She added her soprano voice to our choir.

It took me a moment to respond to her question. I wasn't really giving up, but we were making little progress toward a liver transplant, and Marcia's professional instincts were telling her that time was running out for Maurice.

"I'm going to get Cal right on it!"

At the moment I didn't realize just what that meant. Her husband is a physician who got out of his practice at a rather young age, assuming a new role of helping people work their way through the maze of red tape in the medical system. He was an advocate, and just the kind we needed. I didn't know him well, but that changed rapidly. This man had tenacity. Later the same night Marcia and I were sitting at the bar, ignoring Dr. Atkins and savoring a greasy, delicious pizza (the best in town) at Fricano's Pizza Tavern in Grand Haven. It's a weekly ritual, a time when we spend a few minutes with our youngest son Matthew, who moonlights by tending bar there on Thursday evenings. My late supper was interrupted by a cell phone call. "Doug, it's Cal Dykstra."

The good doctor then informed me what documents he needed from the two hospitals that had treated Maurice in the past three months. He had already prepared release forms for Maurice to sign in order to obtain the documents. In no time I transported the forms to Lamont, and within another day I returned them to Cal bearing Maurice's signatures.

One day later and Cal called again. He also needed the prison medical records. They were stacked on the floor two feet from my desk. He wanted them now. I complied. He spoke with hepatologists, he called representatives at Henry Ford Hospital, and he pored through hospital records and medical reports (some of the ones from prison were hand-written and difficult to decipher). I swear he worked nonstop.

Cal continued at a frantic pace for the next two weeks, preparing a letter of application for a liver transplant evaluation. It had been dictated and was ready to be sent the very morning that Maurice died. It may have been too little too late, but it was a Herculean effort under heavy pressure. While still conscious, Maurice expressed his appreciation. Family members did the same. Marcia and I continue to thank him.

On Friday, October 15, our daughter Tracy Ann, her husband Greg, and baby Cole arrived in Michigan from Hawaii. It was a special moment for our family.

Marcia had stopped at the nursing home to visit Maurice. His legs were swollen, and he was having a difficult time getting dressed, let alone walking.

"We're picking you up on Sunday," she informed Maurice. "We'll give you plenty of time to get ready. You're coming to our house for a family reunion. Jon will be doing the cooking."

Maurice felt like protesting, but his feelings were offset by his incredible desire to see and visit with *all* members of our immediate family.

Picking up Maurice and transporting him anywhere was, by now, no simple task. Our two sons-in-law were exceptionally good at it, and on that Sunday they got the job done.

Maurice with the Tjapkes family, "his" family

Maurice walked very slowly through the front door but broke into his famous wide smile when he saw everyone, and I mean everyone. This was his first time to meet, person to person, Tracy Ann and Greg, and he was then introduced to Cole, not yet one year old. The entire gang was there: Melissa and Matthew along with baby Hannah; Sue and Jon, along with 3-year-old twins Brenden and Zachary; Cindy and Lee, with their growing kids, 12-year-old Betsi and 9-year-old Max; and, of course, Marcia and me.

We had a special reclining/rocking chair reserved for Maurice out in the sun room. Jon was cooking on the outdoor grill right next to him. Maurice watched him in awe. He said to Jon, "You got it *down!*"

(He was supposed to have no appetite. He ate like a horse.)

And then it was time for family pictures. I am so proud that we were able to get one shot, thanks to an automatic shutter, with every member of our immediate family, including Maurice, as we stood, sat, and crouched along one wall in our great room. It's a photograph that we will always treasure.

Maurice was so exhausted that he couldn't stay long, and the farewell ceremony took some time. He never said goodbye without a hug. That meant a lot of hugs.

In all of the busyness and commotion he missed one little last-minute hug, but that embrace didn't escape the attention of Jon and me. Little Zachary, who had a special affection for Maurice, snugged up against his leg and said, "Love you, Maurice." Jon looked at me. Our eyes watered.

On Thursday, October 21, I stopped at the nursing home to see Maurice in the morning because choir rehearsals are on the regular schedule for Thursday evenings. He was hardly conscious. I shook his shoulder several times until his eyes opened. He looked at me, smiled briefly, then closed his eyes.

"Hey, Big Bro!"

"Dr. Dykstra has your application to Ford Hospital ready. We're going to get you a new liver!"

"I'm ready! Are you ready?"

No more conversation. His condition was almost comatose. There was no point in my staying.

I leaned over, touched him again and said loudly, "I love you, man."

I saw that his mouth was moving. I heard the faint whisper: "I love you!" These would be his last words to me.

A few hours later Mary called. Maurice had been rushed to

the Butterworth Campus of Spectrum Health in Grand Rapids once again. No surprise to me. I called Cal Dykstra, who was at his Grand Rapids office. "I'm on my way," he said.

Another Thursday night call at the pizza joint. "Doug, it's Cal." His message surprised me. He was fairly optimistic. The doctors in Spectrum were doing a good job. Cal instructed them to use any means to keep him going, because we were going to try to get him a liver.

I stopped at the hospital Friday morning, but Maurice was too zonked to converse. Then on Friday afternoon there came an ominous message from Mary: "He's on life support."

What? I thought Cal had said he was hanging on! I called Cal, and again he dropped everything and sped to the hospital.

He called me shortly from Butterworth, this time with bad news. Full code. Everything in his body had shut down.

Everything.

Back to the hospital Saturday morning. This time I was instructed to wear protective gear. The nurse who was taking care of him explained to me that every piece of life-saving equipment in this critical care unit was in operation, but things didn't look good. Nothing was stable.

There was no hint of response when I touched Maurice with my gloved hand. I prayed at his bedside in silence.

I didn't return. Sunday was the day for his immediate family to visit. They weren't able to communicate with him, either, but they were able to say their goodbyes.

On Monday morning, the call came from Mary: "Maurice passed."

Jesus wept.

—John 11:35

Among my treasured possessions from the years devoted to seeking justice for my friend are letters written by other treasured friends who fell in step with me on this journey, who guided and supported. Following are excerpts from two.

From Pam Cytrynbaum, program coordinator for Professor David Protess at the Medill Innocence Project:

> Oh God. Oh God.
>
> Here's the hug I can offer. It comes in the words of Sister Helen Prejean, a friend of us all, and, magically, a friend to me while I was in New Orleans covering death penalty cases for the local newspaper. I was covering the grotesque trial of an innocent man, Vernon Williams. The night after he was (inevitably) convicted, I sobbed to Sister Helen. "What can I do? I failed him!"
>
> She asked me, "Have I failed the men I have watched die?'
>
> "Of course not," I said.
>
> "Why?" She asked me.
>
> "Because you never gave up."
>
> She said, "What you have done is to walk beside this man. It is what I do. That is all we can do. Keep walking. Keep on walking beside him. That is our grace."
>
> He was free, Doug. But not merely. You are beside him. He is beside you.
>
> That is your grace. That is his.
>
> My heart is with you both.
>
> Pam

And this, from Phil Campbell, Toronto attorney and AIDWYC board member:

> ... your commitment to Maurice went much, much further than legal advocacy on his behalf.
>
> I wanted to let you know that I am thinking of you. And among the things I have thought is that your work accomplished a great deal. It was decisive in giving Maurice three months of freedom. Those must have been among the sweetest days of his life. It served as an inspiration for countless other people—me among them. And it was ultimately transformative.
>
> The official record shows Maurice to be convicted of attempted murder. But in the eyes of the public, and of many more who studied the case, he achieved exoneration. When you met Maurice he was a forgotten man; he died a celebrity. When you met him he was reviled as a dangerous criminal; he died a symbol of wronged innocence. When you met him he had no real friends; he died surrounded by love.
>
> The qualities he displayed during the bleakest years imaginable are answer enough to his accusers.
>
> I wish you, and Maurice's other friends, his family, and supporters, all the best.
>
> Warmly,
> Phil

TWENTY-THREE

DECEMBER 2004

Christmas morning.

I was alone. I pulled on a pair of jeans and inserted the leather belt that Maurice Carter had given to me. He and Marcia enjoyed teasing me about my waistline as he was making the belt. I'd like to talk to him now, to show him that I had tackled the overweight problem, and was now using the last notch in the belt.

Soon Marcia would be up, and later the house would be filled with gaiety, as grandchildren tore open gifts with abandon.

I made a pot of coffee and stared out at the snow-covered trees.

As I fingered the fine leatherwork on the belt, I reflected on the many years of anticipation, the many words of assurance I had given Maurice Carter that one day, as a free man, he would join us for a joyous Christmas celebration.

It was not to be.

Earlier in the week Reverend Al Hoksbergen and I had dutifully driven to Gary, Indiana, for one more Christmas visit with Maurice's elderly mother, an annual event. This was the year that Maurice and I had planned to make the trip together. And that was not to be, either. Mrs. Fowler wept as I presented her with a picture of mother and son on the day he was freed. She was giving him his first kiss as a free man.

She murmured her agreement as Pastor Al, in our prayer circle, thanked God that Maurice was now in a better place.

I'm going where the wicked shall cease their troubling,
And the weary shall be at rest. [39]

We waved from the car to the sad little woman in the window of the sad little dwelling. Our goodbye was not festive.

Back to Christmas morning. It was difficult to catch what we like to call "the Christmas spirit."

I spotted a small envelope that arrived in the mail the day before. I must have missed it earlier; it was still unopened. The Christmas card was from the Reverend Keith Tanis, that wonderful friend who preached the sermon on the memorable morning when I introduced Maurice Carter to the Ferrysburg congregation.

There was a brief, handwritten note. He always called me "Douger":

"It was an amazing year—Maurice getting outta jail, and then outta here altogether.

"Heaven is closer. Life is precious!

"Keep praising the Christ.

"Drink good wine.

"Laugh a lot."

EPILOGUE

Obviously, there remains another story here. Billy Lee Brown enjoys his freedom. As the Innocence Project's Barry Scheck frequently points out, there are two terrible things about a wrongful conviction. The first is that an innocent man is placed in jail. The second is that the real perpetrator is often still on the street, still committing crimes. I cannot say for certain that Brown is still committing crimes, although those who know him well are quick to say that he has a checkered past.

The tapes, secretly hidden in a safe place without any editing, were a clear indication to those of us working on the investigation that many people know who committed the crime.

One woman whom Pat Shellenbarger interviewed while preparing *The Grand Rapids Press* exposé said she personally heard Brown boasting about shooting "that white cop" at a drinking party. Our courageous Lateesha was unable to get the woman's voice and statement on tape.

Tape number one, the most damning of them all, features an interview with Mama Nana who readily admits that she heard Billy Lee confess to the crime. Other relatives confirmed that she hid the man until enough money could be raised to send him to Ohio.

Tape number two features an interview with Dawg's mother who says it all when she states that the black people know who did it, the white people know, and the police know. Yet no one did anything about it.

Tape number three features an interview with Dawg's uncle, who nervously spoke about the shooting with open fear that Billy Lee might harm him.

Berrien County Prosecutor James Cherry has adamantly refused to reopen the case unless he and his staff speak with Lateesha first, we assume to verify the authenticity of the tapes. We have agreed that he may interview Lateesha, but only if she has counsel present. Grand Rapids attorney Carole Bos has agreed to represent her. These terms, however, are unacceptable to Cherry.

I met in private with two top Michigan State Police officials, one a veteran detective. After reviewing the transcripts they readily agreed that there was more than enough reason to pick up and interview Brown. In fact, they observed that this was already more evidence than authorities went to trial with against Maurice Carter. But they may not initiate an investigation that was not theirs to begin with. So we're back to Cherry again.

I must quickly add that these state cops were not just trying to be nice guys, hoping to clear the record of the late Maurice Carter. They were interested in making an arrest and getting a criminal off the street.

A legal advisor took the transcripts to a confidant who formerly served as a U.S. District Attorney. His reaction was the same. If this had been a federal case, and if he had this much evidence, he said that he would have dispatched members of the FBI to pick up Brown.

So while leading state and federal officials who deal with crime on a regular basis agree that we have a prime suspect, a stubborn county prosecutor continues to block the road.

Another mystery is why the Schadler family is so opposed to this investigation. This became apparent when Lateesha bravely ignored threats and offers of payment. Even though Prosecutor Cherry has implied that he does not know the identity of our informant, one can bet that if Schadlers uncovered the name of Lateesha, that information has been shared with the Prosecutor's office. In fact, a recent series of unpleasant incidents involving Lateesha and the Berrien County judicial system would almost indicate that she is and has been the victim of unnecessary harassment. Pat Shellenbarger, Carole Bos, and I agree that her burden is heavy. I pray for this single mom regularly, that Jesus might share her weighty load as he has promised.

There's still another issue, and that is the criminal charge. The charge against Maurice Carter, assault with intent to murder, has a statue of limitations that has expired. A savvy state police detective said, however, that if it were his case and his call, he would seek a charge of attempted murder (which has no statute) because the shooter deliberately aimed at the back of the head of a victim when he fired the shots.

We are not letting this frustrating set of circumstances stop us. We continue knocking on doors. The problem is that potential witnesses are getting older, and some have already died. Our goal, as well as that of the police, is to see that justice is finally done.

It goes without question that we would love to see the record of Maurice Carter cleared. But as Canadian barrister Phil Campbell so eloquently pointed out, his name was already cleared. This victim of the system spent nearly thirty years behind bars, and while there picked up enough bad germs to bring an early end to his life. But to all who knew and loved him, Maurice Carter was an innocent man.

1. Matthew 25:37
2. "Oh Be Careful Little Ears," Sunday School Song, Unknown.
3. Affidavit of Peter Perdomo, polygraph examiner, was an exhibit in the documents filed in Berrien County Circuit Court by the legal team. The affidavit was notarized April 11, 2002, in the State of South Carolina, County of Anderson.
4. "I'll be a Sunbeam," Sunday School Song written by Nellie Talbot, circa 1900.
5. "God Moves in a Mysterious Way," Peom written by William Cowper, 1779.
6. "His Eye Is On the Sparrow," Words by Mrs. Civilla D. Martin, Melody by Charles Hutchinson Gabriel.
7. Letter from Paul L. Maloney, former prosecuting attorney, Berrien County, to the state attorney general. Copies had been provided to Maurice Carter either by request or by FOIA filing by the Michigan Parole Board to justify its rejection of parole.
8. Legendary hero in Lawrence Sanders novel series.
9. "Swing Down, Sweet Chariot," Traditional Spiritual.
10. Lyrics derived from Charles Tindley's gospel song, "I'll Overcome Some Day," (1900).
11. "This Little Light of Mine" (Version 2), Composer unknown, Copyright unknown.
12. State of Michigan, Attorney Discipline Board, Notice of Suspension and Restitution, Case Numbers 92-199-GA; 92-233-FA Suspension, 35 days, effective March 1, 1993.
13. State of Michigan, Attorney Discipline Board, Order of Suspension (Issued by Attorney Discipline Board Kalamazoo County Hearing Panel #2), Case #99-062-GA. License of Mr. Jesse suspended "for a period of 45 days commencing March 20, 2000."
14. Documents from State of Michigan Attorney Grievance Commission.
15. "Another try at justice: Maurice Carter deserves a new trial in Berrien County," Ed Golder, editorial page, *The Grand Rapids Press*, Monday, June 9, 2003.
16. "Nobody Knows the Trouble I've Seen," Traditional Spiritual, Unknown.

17. "Deep and Wide," Sunday School Song, Unknown.
18. "Fury within community a sad, historic refrain," David Zeman, *Free Press* staff writer, *Detroit Free Press*, June 19, 2003.
19. "Biker barristers hit the road to help U.S. inmate," Tracey Tyler and Harold Levy, staff reporters, *Toronto Star*, June 28, 2003.
20. "Ain't Gonna Study War No More," Traditional Spiritual, Unknown.
21. "Biker barristers hit the road to help U.S. inmate," Tracey Tyler and Harold Levy, staff reporters, *Toronto Star*, June 28, 2003.
22. "'Hurricane' Carter tried to calm a city caught in violence," Clyde Hughes, *Blade* staff writer, *Toledo Blade*, June 20, 2003.
23. Pat Shellenbarger's words to Doug Tpjakes following the November 12, 2003 hearing.
24. *Eric Zorn's Notebook*, a web log by *Chicago Tribune* columnist Eric Zorn, Thursday, October 30, 2003, last updated at 12:41 p.m.
25. "A case of bad judgment: Berrien judge shows bias against man seeking retrial," Ed Golder, editorial page, *The Grand Rapids Press*, November 3, 2003.
26. "Send in the Clowns," words and music by Stephen Sondheim, from the musical *A Little Night Music*.
27. "Sweet Little Jesus Boy," by Robert MacGimsey.
28. "Justice goes up in smoke along with new trial," Eric Zorn, *Chicago Tribune* online edition, November 13, 2003.
29. God on the Mountain, by Tracy G. Dartt, Gaviota Music (a div. of Manna Music, Inc.), copyright 1988.
30. "Go, Tell It on the Mountains," Traditional American Folk Song.
31. "The appalling coward who sits in the governor's office in Michigan," *Eric Zorn's Notebook*, chicagotribune.com web log, Thursday, March 18, 2004.
32. "There Is a Balm in Gilead," African American Spiritual.
33. Dr. Martin Luther King, Jr., Letter from Birmingham Jail, April 16, 1963.
34. "Master, the Tempest is Raging," Music by Horatio R. Palmer, Words by Mary A. Baker, 1874.
35. Eternal Life, Olive Dungan (St. Francis of Assisi).
36. Old Negro spiritual, quoted by Dr. King in "I Have a Dream" speech.
37. Dr. Martin Luther King, from a speech for the Southern Christian Leadership Conference in Atlanta, GA, August 16, 1967.
38. "God Is So Good," African Christian Folk Song (public domain).
39. "The Wicked Shall Cease Their Troubling," Spiritual, Unknown.

ABOUT THE AUTHOR

Douglas John Tjapkes was born to John and Mary Tjapkes during a blustery November snowstorm in Muskegon, Michigan, in the year 1936.

Many of Doug's activities, milestones, and mild accomplishments came at relatively early ages. For example:

–starting piano lessons at age 4 ("If you're going to keep banging on that piano you might as well learn where the notes are!")

–first radio program, Calling All Kids!, at age twelve ("You're always imitating radio announcers, why not call WKNK and see if they'll give you an audition?")

–youngest radio news director in Grand Rapids market at age nineteen

–general manager of a radio station with fifteen employees at age twenty-six

–president and general manager of his own radio station at age twenty-seven

–winner of national broadcast editorial writer competition in his mid-thirties.

Doug has had three careers, the first as a radio broadcaster (1954–1983); the second as a church organ salesman (1983–2004); and now the third as president of INNOCENT!, an inmate advocacy organization specializing in helping the wrongly convicted.

His avocation is Christian music.

His hobby is racing Studebakers.

In his careers he won several radio writing awards, sold hundreds of organs to churches in western Michigan, and participated in the effort to free Maurice Carter.

In his avocation, he served his church for more than forty years as a pianist, organist, and choir director; he accompanied a singing duo in a regular radio broadcast whose travels took him as far away as Viet Nam; and he directed a male chorus whose ministry focused on prisons and led to singing tours around the nation and overseas to the Caribbean.

In his hobby, he purchased a Studebaker truck in the state of Washington and drove it home through the mountains and across the prairies; and regularly drag-races a 1963 Studebaker Super Hawk.

The list of failures, foolish mistakes, and disappointments in the life of Doug Tjapkes would require an even larger page, but shall be ignored.

Doug and his wife Marcia reside in Spring Lake, Michigan, where they often can be heard boasting about their four wonderful children and six delightful grandchildren.